Fairhaven Media

FAIRHAVEN MEDIA

MY HOUSE
Copyright 2020 © by Hubert and Sheila Robertson

All rights reserved. No part of this publication may be reproduced, stored in a retrieval system, or transmitted in any form or by any means—electronic, mechanical, photocopy, recording, or any other—except for brief quotations in printed reviews, without the prior permission of the   publisher.

Cover by: Izzit Graphics www.izzitgraphics.com
Interior Layout: Sheila Robertson
Character designs: Jennifer Pettyjohn

Printed in the United States of America

ISBN: 978-1-947729-08-7
Home, House records, Home repairs

Welcome to

We hope you will enjoy using this book to record all the history of your house. This book is intended to stay with the house as it passes from one owner to the next.

When the new owner receives this treasure chest of information about their new home, they will be thrilled to have a complete history of the house.

Hopefully, when you buy your next home, there will also be a MY HOUSE book awaiting you. If not, then you can start the tradition for your new home by filling in all the information that you possibly can in a new volume of MY HOUSE.

Remember, don't get stressed out if you can't provide all the information that is contained in this book. Be as thorough as you can, and this volume will provide a valuable record for you of all the systems in your house and the work performed.

Hi! I'm Homer Homeowner and I'll be your guide through this adventure.
Here we go!

Table of Contents

General House Info	6
Homeowners	7
House Systems	11
Water	12
Sewer	16
Gas	20
HVAC	26
Generator	32
Central Vacuum	33
Water Filtration	34
Internet	35
Cable	37
Phone	39
Plumbing	41
Electrical Repair & Fixtures	55
Appliances	75
Painting	117
Floor Covering	159
Exterior	179
Remodels	201

GENERAL HOME INFO

Address
_____

City, State, Zip
_____

Subdivision
_____

Lot #
_____

Builder Name
_____

Builder Contact Info
_____

Platt #
_____

Deed #
_____

Tax Card #
_____

HOME OWNERS

Name | Original owner ☐ Yes ☐ No

Date Purchased | optional Purchase $

Date moved in | Date moved out

Name

Date Purchased | optional Purchase $

Date moved in | Date moved out

Name

Date Purchased | optional Purchase $

Date moved in | Date moved out

Name

Date Purchased | optional Purchase $

Date moved in | Date moved out

HOME OWNERS

Name
_____

Date Purchased   optional
                        Purchase $
_____

Date moved in   Date moved out
_____

Name
_____

Date Purchased   optional
                        Purchase $
_____

Date moved in   Date moved out
_____

Name
_____

Date Purchased   optional
                        Purchase $
_____

Date moved in   Date moved out
_____

Name
_____

Date Purchased   optional
                        Purchase $
_____

Date moved in   Date moved out
_____

HOME OWNERS

Name
_____

Date Purchased _____ optional Purchase $ _____

Date moved in _____ Date moved out _____

Name
_____

Date Purchased _____ optional Purchase $ _____

Date moved in _____ Date moved out _____

Name
_____

Date Purchased _____ optional Purchase $ _____

Date moved in _____ Date moved out _____

Name
_____

Date Purchased _____ optional Purchase $ _____

Date moved in _____ Date moved out _____

HOME OWNERS

Name _____

Date Purchased _____ optional Purchase $ _____

Date moved in _____ Date moved out _____

Name _____

Date Purchased _____ optional Purchase $ _____

Date moved in _____ Date moved out _____

Name _____

Date Purchased _____ optional Purchase $ _____

Date moved in _____ Date moved out _____

Name _____

Date Purchased _____ optional Purchase $ _____

Date moved in _____ Date moved out _____

House Systems

Fun Fact
Willis Carrier is generally credited with producing the first air conditioning system.

Helpful Hint
Clean or replace your filters regularly. A dirty, clogged filter can not only lower your HVAC unit's efficiency, it can cause undue wear and tear on your equipment.

Water System—MAIN SUPPLY

Original Hook up _____ Date _____

Materials: *(i.e. pvc, copper, pex, etc.)* _____

Installed by _____

Repairs _____

Repairs made by: _____

Repairman contact info _____

Notes

Repairs _____ Date _____

Repairs made by: _____

Repairman contact info _____

Notes

Repairs _____ Date _____

Repairs made by: _____

Repairman contact info _____

Notes

Water System— Hot & Cold Supply Lines

Original Hook up _____ Date _____

Materials: *(i.e. pvc, copper, pex, etc.)* _____

Installed by _____

Repairs _____

Repairs made by: _____

Repairman contact info _____

Notes

Repairs _____ Date _____

Repairs made by: _____

Repairman contact info _____

Notes

Repairs _____ Date _____

Repairs made by: _____

Repairman contact info _____

Notes

Water System—Shut Off

LOCATION _____

Original Hook up _____ Date _____

Installed by _____

Repairs _____ Date _____

Repairs made by: _____

Repairman contact info _____

Notes
```
                                        
                                        
                                        
```

Repairs _____ Date _____

Repairs made by: _____

Repairman contact info _____

Notes
```
                                        
                                        
                                        
```

Repairs _____ Date _____

Repairs made by: _____

Repairman contact info _____

Notes
```
                                        
                                        
                                        
```

Water System— Valves & Hook ups

Original Hook up _____ Date _____

Materials: *(i.e. pvc, copper, pex, etc.)* _____

Installed by _____

Repairs _____

Repairs made by: _____

Repairman contact info _____

Notes

Repairs _____ Date _____

Repairs made by: _____

Repairman contact info _____

Notes

Repairs _____ Date _____

Repairs made by: _____

Repairman contact info _____

Notes

CITY SEWER

Original Hook up _____ Date _____

Materials: *(i.e. pvc, copper, pex, etc.)* _____

Installed by _____

Exit LOCATION _____

Clean Out LOCATION _____

Notes

Repairs _____ Date _____

Repairs made by: _____

Repairman contact info _____

Notes

Repairs _____ Date _____

Repairs made by: _____

Repairman contact info _____

Notes

CITY SEWER

Repairs _____ Date _____

Repairs made by: _____

Repairman contact info _____

Notes

Repairs _____ Date _____

Repairs made by: _____

Repairman contact info _____

Notes

Repairs _____ Date _____

Repairs made by: _____

Repairman contact info _____

Notes

Repairs _____ Date _____

Repairs made by: _____

Repairman contact info _____

Notes

SEPTIC TANK

Original Hook up _____ Date _____

Installed by _____

Tank LOCATION _____

Field Line LOCATION _____

Notes

Repairs _____ Date _____

Repairs made by: _____

Repairman contact info _____

Notes

Repairs _____ Date _____

Repairs made by: _____

Repairman contact info _____

Notes

SEPTIC TANK

Repairs _____ Date _____

Repairs made by: _____

Repairman contact info _____

Notes

Repairs _____ Date _____

Repairs made by: _____

Repairman contact info _____

Notes

Repairs _____ Date _____

Repairs made by: _____

Repairman contact info _____

Notes

Repairs _____ Date _____

Repairs made by: _____

Repairman contact info _____

Notes

Gas Lines

Original Hook up _____ Date _____

Installed by _____ Natural Gas ☐
                                       Propane Gas ☐

Materials: *(i.e. pvc, copper, pex, etc.)* _____

Repairs _____

Repairs made by: _____

Repairman contact info _____

Notes

Repairs _____ Date _____

Repairs made by: _____

Repairman contact info _____

Notes

Repairs _____ Date _____

Repairs made by: _____

Repairman contact info _____

Notes

Gas Fireplace Logs

ROOM LOCATION _____ Original to the house ☐ Yes ☐ No

Installed by _____ Date _____

Materials: *(i.e. black iron, galvanized etc.)* _____

Repairs _____

Repairs made by: _____

Repairman contact info _____

Notes

Repairs _____ Date _____

Repairs made by: _____

Repairman contact info _____

Notes

Repairs _____ Date _____

Repairs made by: _____

Repairman contact info _____

Notes

Gas Fireplace Logs

ROOM LOCATION _____ Original to the house ☐ Yes ☐ No

Installed by _____ Date _____

Materials: *(i.e. black iron, galvanized etc.)* _____

Repairs _____

Repairs made by: _____

Repairman contact info _____

Notes
```

```

Repairs _____ Date _____

Repairs made by: _____

Repairman contact info _____

Notes
```

```

Repairs _____ Date _____

Repairs made by: _____

Repairman contact info _____

Notes
```

```

Gas Fireplace Logs

ROOM LOCATION _____ Original to the house ☐ Yes ☐ No

Installed by _____ Date _____

Materials: *(i.e. black iron, galvanized etc.)* _____

Repairs _____

Repairs made by: _____

Repairman contact info _____

Notes

Repairs _____ Date _____

Repairs made by: _____

Repairman contact info _____

Notes

Repairs _____ Date _____

Repairs made by: _____

Repairman contact info _____

Notes

Gas Heater

ROOM LOCATION _____ Original to the house ☐ Yes ☐ No

Installed by _____ Date _____

Materials: *(i.e. black iron, galvanized etc.)* _____

Repairs _____

Repairs made by: _____

Repairman contact info _____

Notes

Repairs _____ Date _____

Repairs made by: _____

Repairman contact info _____

Notes

Repairs _____ Date _____

Repairs made by: _____

Repairman contact info _____

Notes

Gas Heater

ROOM LOCATION _____ Original to the house ☐ Yes ☐ No

Installed by _____ Date _____

Materials: *(i.e. black iron, galvanized etc.)* _____

Repairs _____

Repairs made by: _____

Repairman contact info _____

Notes

Repairs _____ Date _____

Repairs made by: _____

Repairman contact info _____

Notes

Repairs _____ Date _____

Repairs made by: _____

Repairman contact info _____

Notes

HVAC SYSTEM

BRAND _____ Date Installed _____

Unit size _____

Type of system   ☐ Natural Gas   ☐ LP Gas   ☐ Electric _____

☐ Other—explain _____

Installed by _____

Installers contact info _____

Notes

Repairs _____ Date _____

Repairs made by: _____

Repairman contact info _____

Notes

Repairs _____ Date _____

Repairs made by: _____

Repairman contact info _____

Notes

HVAC cont'd

Repairs _____ Date _____

Repairs made by: _____

Repairman contact info _____

Notes

Repairs _____ Date _____

Repairs made by: _____

Repairman contact info _____

Notes

Repairs _____ Date _____

Repairs made by: _____

Repairman contact info _____

Notes

Repairs _____ Date _____

Repairs made by: _____

Repairman contact info _____

Notes

HVAC SYSTEM #2

BRAND _____ Date Installed _____

Unit size _____

Type of system   ☐ Natural Gas   ☐ LP Gas   ☐ Electric

☐ Other—explain _____

Installed by _____

Installers contact info _____

Notes
```
```

Repairs _____ Date _____

Repairs made by: _____

Repairman contact info _____

Notes
```
```

Repairs _____ Date _____

Repairs made by: _____

Repairman contact info _____

Notes
```
```

HVAC #2 cont'd

Repairs _____ Date _____

Repairs made by: _____

Repairman contact info _____

Notes

Repairs _____ Date _____

Repairs made by: _____

Repairman contact info _____

Notes

Repairs _____ Date _____

Repairs made by: _____

Repairman contact info _____

Notes

Repairs _____ Date _____

Repairs made by: _____

Repairman contact info _____

Notes

HVAC SYSTEM #3

BRAND _____ Date Installed _____

Unit size _____

Type of system ☐ Natural Gas   ☐ LP Gas   ☐ Electric

☐ Other—explain _____

Installed by _____

Installers contact info _____

Notes

Repairs _____ Date _____

Repairs made by: _____

Repairman contact info _____

Notes

Repairs _____ Date _____

Repairs made by: _____

Repairman contact info _____

Notes

HVAC #3 cont'd

Repairs _____ Date _____

Repairs made by: _____

Repairman contact info _____

Notes

Repairs _____ Date _____

Repairs made by: _____

Repairman contact info _____

Notes

Repairs _____ Date _____

Repairs made by: _____

Repairman contact info _____

Notes

Repairs _____ Date _____

Repairs made by: _____

Repairman contact info _____

Notes

GENERATOR

BRAND _____ Purchased from _____ Date _____

Generator kw size _____ Fuel Type _____

Installed by _____

Repairs _____

Repairs made by: _____

Repairman contact info _____

Notes

Repairs _____ Date _____

Repairs made by: _____

Repairman contact info _____

Notes

Repairs _____ Date _____

Repairs made by: _____

Repairman contact info _____

Notes

Central Vacuum

BRAND _____ Date Purchased _____

Purchased from _____

Installed by _____

Repairs _____

Repairs made by: _____

Repairman contact info _____

Notes

Repairs _____ Date _____

Repairs made by: _____

Repairman contact info _____

Notes

Repairs _____ Date _____

Repairs made by: _____

Repairman contact info _____

Notes

Water Filtration

BRAND _____ Date Purchased _____

Purchased from _____

Installed by _____

Repairs _____

Repairs made by: _____

Repairman contact info _____

Notes

Repairs _____ Date _____

Repairs made by: _____

Repairman contact info _____

Notes

Repairs _____ Date _____

Repairs made by: _____

Repairman contact info _____

Notes

INTERNET

Provider _____ Date _____

Installed by _____

Repairs _____

Repairs made by: _____

Repairman contact info _____

Notes

Repairs _____ Date _____

Repairs made by: _____

Repairman contact info _____

Notes

Repairs _____ Date _____

Repairs made by: _____

Repairman contact info _____

Notes

INTERNET

Repairs _____ Date _____

Repairs made by: _____

Repairman contact info _____

Notes
```

```

Repairs _____ Date _____

Repairs made by: _____

Repairman contact info _____

Notes
```

```

Repairs _____ Date _____

Repairs made by: _____

Repairman contact info _____

Notes
```

```

Repairs _____ Date _____

Repairs made by: _____

Repairman contact info _____

Notes
```

```

CABLE

Provider _____ Date _____

Installed by _____

Repairs _____

Repairs made by: _____

Repairman contact info _____

Notes

Repairs _____ Date _____

Repairs made by: _____

Repairman contact info _____

Notes

Repairs _____ Date _____

Repairs made by: _____

Repairman contact info _____

Notes

CABLE

Repairs _____ Date _____

Repairs made by: _____

Repairman contact info _____

Notes

Repairs _____ Date _____

Repairs made by: _____

Repairman contact info _____

Notes

Repairs _____ Date _____

Repairs made by: _____

Repairman contact info _____

Notes

Repairs _____ Date _____

Repairs made by: _____

Repairman contact info _____

Notes

PHONE

Provider _____ Date _____

Installed by _____

Repairs _____

Repairs made by: _____

Repairman contact info _____

Notes

Repairs _____ Date _____

Repairs made by: _____

Repairman contact info _____

Notes

Repairs _____ Date _____

Repairs made by: _____

Repairman contact info _____

Notes

PHONE

Repairs _____ Date _____

Repairs made by: _____

Repairman contact info _____

Notes

Repairs _____ Date _____

Repairs made by: _____

Repairman contact info _____

Notes

Repairs _____ Date _____

Repairs made by: _____

Repairman contact info _____

Notes

Repairs _____ Date _____

Repairs made by: _____

Repairman contact info _____

Notes

Plumbing

Fun Fact
Earthen plumbing pipes with asphalt seals were in use in the Indus valley by 2700 B.C.

Helpful Hint
Always turn off the main shut off valve before attempting any plumbing repair.

Plumbing Fixtures

Room Name   Date Purchased

Fixture Replaced   Price $

Brand

Installed by

Installers contact info

Notes

Room Name   Date Purchased

Fixture Replaced   Price $

Brand

Installed by

Installers contact info

Notes

Room Name   Date Purchased

Fixture Replaced   Price $

Brand

Installed by

Installers contact info

Notes

Plumbing Fixtures

Room Name _____ Date Purchased _____

Fixture Replaced _____ Price $ _____

Brand _____

Installed by _____

Installers contact info _____

Notes

Room Name _____ Date Purchased _____

Fixture Replaced _____ Price $ _____

Brand _____

Installed by _____

Installers contact info _____

Notes

Room Name _____ Date Purchased _____

Fixture Replaced _____ Price $ _____

Brand _____

Installed by _____

Installers contact info _____

Notes

Plumbing Fixtures

Room Name   Date Purchased

Fixture Replaced   Price $

Brand

Installed by

Installers contact info

Notes

Room Name   Date Purchased

Fixture Replaced   Price $

Brand

Installed by

Installers contact info

Notes

Room Name   Date Purchased

Fixture Replaced   Price $

Brand

Installed by

Installers contact info

Notes

Plumbing Fixtures

Room Name Date Purchased

Fixture Replaced Price $

Brand

Installed by

Installers contact info

Notes

Room Name Date Purchased

Fixture Replaced Price $

Brand

Installed by

Installers contact info

Notes

Room Name Date Purchased

Fixture Replaced Price $

Brand

Installed by

Installers contact info

Notes

Plumbing Fixtures

Room Name _____ Date Purchased _____

Fixture Replaced _____ Price $ _____

Brand _____

Installed by _____

Installers contact info _____

Notes

Room Name _____ Date Purchased _____

Fixture Replaced _____ Price $ _____

Brand _____

Installed by _____

Installers contact info _____

Notes

Room Name _____ Date Purchased _____

Fixture Replaced _____ Price $ _____

Brand _____

Installed by _____

Installers contact info _____

Notes

Plumbing Fixtures

Room Name Date Purchased

Fixture Replaced Price $

Brand

Installed by

Installers contact info

Notes

Room Name Date Purchased

Fixture Replaced Price $

Brand

Installed by

Installers contact info

Notes

Room Name Date Purchased

Fixture Replaced Price $

Brand

Installed by

Installers contact info

Notes

Plumbing Fixtures

Room Name   Date Purchased

Fixture Replaced   Price $

Brand

Installed by

Installers contact info

Notes

Room Name   Date Purchased

Fixture Replaced   Price $

Brand

Installed by

Installers contact info

Notes

Room Name   Date Purchased

Fixture Replaced   Price $

Brand

Installed by

Installers contact info

Notes

Plumbing Fixtures

Room Name   Date Purchased

Fixture Replaced   Price $

Brand

Installed by

Installers contact info

Notes

Room Name   Date Purchased

Fixture Replaced   Price $

Brand

Installed by

Installers contact info

Notes

Room Name   Date Purchased

Fixture Replaced   Price $

Brand

Installed by

Installers contact info

Notes

Plumbing Fixtures

Room Name _____ Date Purchased _____

Fixture Replaced _____ Price $ _____

Brand _____

Installed by _____

Installers contact info _____

Notes

Room Name _____ Date Purchased _____

Fixture Replaced _____ Price $ _____

Brand _____

Installed by _____

Installers contact info _____

Notes

Room Name _____ Date Purchased _____

Fixture Replaced _____ Price $ _____

Brand _____

Installed by _____

Installers contact info _____

Notes

Plumbing Fixtures

Room Name　　　　　　　　　　Date Purchased

Fixture Replaced　　　　　　　　　　Price $

Brand

Installed by

Installers contact info

Notes

Room Name　　　　　　　　　　Date Purchased

Fixture Replaced　　　　　　　　　　Price $

Brand

Installed by

Installers contact info

Notes

Room Name　　　　　　　　　　Date Purchased

Fixture Replaced　　　　　　　　　　Price $

Brand

Installed by

Installers contact info

Notes

Plumbing Fixtures

Room Name _____ Date Purchased _____

Fixture Replaced _____ Price $ _____

Brand _____

Installed by _____

Installers contact info _____

Notes

Room Name _____ Date Purchased _____

Fixture Replaced _____ Price $ _____

Brand _____

Installed by _____

Installers contact info _____

Notes

Room Name _____ Date Purchased _____

Fixture Replaced _____ Price $ _____

Brand _____

Installed by _____

Installers contact info _____

Notes

Plumbing Fixtures

Room Name _____ Date Purchased _____

Fixture Replaced _____ Price $ _____

Brand _____

Installed by _____

Installers contact info _____

Notes

Room Name _____ Date Purchased _____

Fixture Replaced _____ Price $ _____

Brand _____

Installed by _____

Installers contact info _____

Notes

Room Name _____ Date Purchased _____

Fixture Replaced _____ Price $ _____

Brand _____

Installed by _____

Installers contact info _____

Notes

Plumbing Fixtures

Room Name   Date Purchased

Fixture Replaced   Price $

Brand

Installed by

Installers contact info

Notes

Room Name   Date Purchased

Fixture Replaced   Price $

Brand

Installed by

Installers contact info

Notes

Room Name   Date Purchased

Fixture Replaced   Price $

Brand

Installed by

Installers contact info

Notes

Electrical Repair & Fixtures

Fun Fact
The first practical incandescent light bulb was invented by Thomas Edison in 1878.

Helpful Hint
Never attempt any repair or replacement for which you are not qualified. This could result in serious injury or death. Additionally, you may run afoul of your local codes department, not to mention serious damage could occur to your home.

ELECTRICAL Repairs

Room Name　　　　　　　　　　　　Date

Problem

Work performed

Repaired by

Repairman contact info

Notes

Room Name　　　　　　　　　　　　Date

Problem

Work performed

Repaired by

Repairman contact info

Notes

ELECTRICAL Repairs

Room Name _____ Date _____

Problem _____

Work performed _____

Repaired by _____

Repairman contact info _____

Notes

Room Name _____ Date _____

Problem _____

Work performed _____

Repaired by _____

Repairman contact info _____

Notes

ELECTRICAL Repairs

Room Name   Date

Problem

Work performed

Repaired by

Repairman contact info

Notes

Room Name   Date

Problem

Work performed

Repaired by

Repairman contact info

Notes

ELECTRICAL Repairs

Room Name　　　　　　　　　　　　　Date

Problem

Work performed

Repaired by

Repairman contact info

Notes

Room Name　　　　　　　　　　　　　Date

Problem

Work performed

Repaired by

Repairman contact info

Notes

ELECTRICAL Repairs

Room Name   Date

Problem

Work performed

Repaired by

Repairman contact info

Notes

Room Name   Date

Problem

Work performed

Repaired by

Repairman contact info

Notes

ELECTRICAL Repairs

Room Name   Date

Problem

Work performed

Repaired by

Repairman contact info

Notes

Room Name   Date

Problem

Work performed

Repaired by

Repairman contact info

Notes

ELECTRICAL Repairs

Room Name _____ Date _____

Problem _____

Work performed _____

Repaired by _____

Repairman contact info _____

```
Notes



```

Room Name _____ Date _____

Problem _____

Work performed _____

Repaired by _____

Repairman contact info _____

```
Notes



```

ELECTRICAL Repairs

Room Name _____ Date _____

Problem _____

Work performed _____

Repaired by _____

Repairman contact info _____

Notes
```


```

Room Name _____ Date _____

Problem _____

Work performed _____

Repaired by _____

Repairman contact info _____

Notes

Light Fixtures

Room Name _____ Purchased at _____

Brand _____ Date _____ Price $ _____

Installed by _____

Installers contact info _____
Notes

Room Name _____ Purchased at _____

Brand _____ Date _____ Price $ _____

Installed by _____

Installers contact info _____
Notes

Room Name _____ Purchased at _____

Brand _____ Date _____ Price $ _____

Installed by _____

Installers contact info _____
Notes

Light Fixtures

Room Name _____ Purchased at _____

Brand _____ Date _____ Price $ _____

Installed by _____

Installers contact info _____

Notes

Room Name _____ Purchased at _____

Brand _____ Date _____ Price $ _____

Installed by _____

Installers contact info _____

Notes

Room Name _____ Purchased at _____

Brand _____ Date _____ Price $ _____

Installed by _____

Installers contact info _____

Notes

Light Fixtures

Room Name _____ Purchased at _____

Brand _____ Date _____ Price $ _____

Installed by _____

Installers contact info _____

Notes

Room Name _____ Purchased at _____

Brand _____ Date _____ Price $ _____

Installed by _____

Installers contact info _____

Notes

Room Name _____ Purchased at _____

Brand _____ Date _____ Price $ _____

Installed by _____

Installers contact info _____

Notes

Light Fixtures

Room Name   Purchased at

Brand   Date   Price $

Installed by

Installers contact info

Notes

Room Name   Purchased at

Brand   Date   Price $

Installed by

Installers contact info

Notes

Room Name   Purchased at

Brand   Date   Price $

Installed by

Installers contact info

Notes

Light Fixtures

Room Name _____ Purchased at _____

Brand _____ Date _____ Price $ _____

Installed by _____

Installers contact info _____

Notes

Room Name _____ Purchased at _____

Brand _____ Date _____ Price $ _____

Installed by _____

Installers contact info _____

Notes

Room Name _____ Purchased at _____

Brand _____ Date _____ Price $ _____

Installed by _____

Installers contact info _____

Notes

Light Fixtures

Room Name   Purchased at

Brand   Date   Price $

Installed by

Installers contact info

Notes

Room Name   Purchased at

Brand   Date   Price $

Installed by

Installers contact info

Notes

Room Name   Purchased at

Brand   Date   Price $

Installed by

Installers contact info

Notes

Light Fixtures

Room Name   Purchased at

Brand   Date   Price $

Installed by

Installers contact info

Notes

Room Name   Purchased at

Brand   Date   Price $

Installed by

Installers contact info

Notes

Room Name   Purchased at

Brand   Date   Price $

Installed by

Installers contact info

Notes

Light Fixtures

Room Name _____ Purchased at _____

Brand _____ Date _____ Price $ _____

Installed by _____

Installers contact info _____

Notes

Room Name _____ Purchased at _____

Brand _____ Date _____ Price $ _____

Installed by _____

Installers contact info _____

Notes

Room Name _____ Purchased at _____

Brand _____ Date _____ Price $ _____

Installed by _____

Installers contact info _____

Notes

Light Fixtures

Room Name _____ Purchased at _____

Brand _____ Date _____ Price $ _____

Installed by _____

Installers contact info _____
Notes

Room Name _____ Purchased at _____

Brand _____ Date _____ Price $ _____

Installed by _____

Installers contact info _____
Notes

Room Name _____ Purchased at _____

Brand _____ Date _____ Price $ _____

Installed by _____

Installers contact info _____
Notes

Light Fixtures

Room Name _____ Purchased at _____

Brand _____ Date _____ Price $ _____

Installed by _____

Installers contact info _____
Notes

Room Name _____ Purchased at _____

Brand _____ Date _____ Price $ _____

Installed by _____

Installers contact info _____
Notes

Room Name _____ Purchased at _____

Brand _____ Date _____ Price $ _____

Installed by _____

Installers contact info _____
Notes

Light Fixtures

Room Name_____Purchased at_____

Brand_____Date_____Price $_____

Installed by_____

Installers contact info_____

Notes

Room Name_____Purchased at_____

Brand_____Date_____Price $_____

Installed by_____

Installers contact info_____

Notes

Room Name_____Purchased at_____

Brand_____Date_____Price $_____

Installed by_____

Installers contact info_____

Notes

Appliances

Fun Fact
Although artificial refrigeration dates back to the 1750's, the first self-contained home refrigerator was introduced by Frigidaire in 1925.

Helpful Hint
Only use a UL rated appliance extension cord for retrigerator, freezers, microwaves, etc.

Refrigerator

Brand _____ Date _____

Purchased From _____ Price $ _____

Installed by _____

Repairs _____

Repairs made by: _____

Repairman contact info _____

Notes

Brand _____ Date _____

Purchased From _____ Price $ _____

Repairs _____

_____

Repairs made by: _____

Repairman contact info _____

Notes

Refrigerator left with house? ☐ YES ☐ NO

Refrigerator

Brand _____ Date _____

Purchased From _____ Price $ _____

Installed by _____

Repairs _____

Repairs made by: _____

Repairman contact info _____

Notes
```


```

Brand _____ Date _____

Purchased From _____ Price $ _____

Repairs _____

_____

Repairs made by: _____

Repairman contact info _____

Notes
```


```

Refrigerator left with house? ☐ YES ☐ NO

Refrigerator

Brand _____ Date _____

Purchased From _____ Price $ _____

Installed by _____

Repairs _____

Repairs made by: _____

Repairman contact info _____

Notes
```
```

Brand _____ Date _____

Purchased From _____ Price $ _____

Repairs _____
_____

Repairs made by: _____

Repairman contact info _____

Notes
```
```

Refrigerator left with house? ☐ YES   ☐ NO

Stove

Brand _____ Date _____ ☐ Electric ☐ Gas ☐ LP ☐ Natural

Purchased From _____ Price $ _____

Installed by _____

Repairs _____

Repairs made by: _____

Repairman contact info _____

Notes
```


```

Brand _____ Date _____

Purchased From _____ Price $ _____

Repairs _____

_____

Repairs made by: _____

Repairman contact info _____

Notes
```


```

Stove left with house? ☐ YES ☐ NO

Stove

Brand _____ Date _____ ☐ Electric ☐ Gas ☐ LP / ☐ Natural

Purchased From _____ Price $ _____

Installed by _____

Repairs _____

Repairs made by: _____

Repairman contact info _____

Notes
```
┌─────────────────────────────────────────┐
│                                         │
│                                         │
│                                         │
└─────────────────────────────────────────┘
```

Brand _____ Date _____

Purchased From _____ Price $ _____

Repairs _____
_____

Repairs made by: _____

Repairman contact info _____

Notes
```
┌─────────────────────────────────────────┐
│                                         │
│                                         │
│                                         │
└─────────────────────────────────────────┘
```

Stove left with house?   ☐ YES   ☐ NO

Stove

Brand _____ Date _____ ☐ Electric ☐ Gas ☐ LP ☐ Natural

Purchased From _____ Price $ _____

Installed by _____

Repairs _____

Repairs made by: _____

Repairman contact info _____

Notes

Brand _____ Date _____

Purchased From _____ Price $ _____

Repairs _____

_____

Repairs made by: _____

Repairman contact info _____

Notes

Stove left with house? ☐ YES ☐ NO

Cooktop

Brand _____ Date _____ ☐ Electric ☐ Gas ☐ LP ☐ Natural

Purchased From _____ Price $ _____

Installed by _____

Repairs _____

Repairs made by: _____

Repairman contact info _____

Notes
```
















```

Brand _____ Date _____

Purchased From _____ Price $ _____

Repairs _____

_____

Repairs made by: _____

Repairman contact info _____

Notes
```
















```

Cooktop

Brand _____ Date _____ ☐ Electric ☐ Gas ☐ LP ☐ Natural

Purchased From _____ Price $ _____

Installed by _____

Repairs _____

Repairs made by: _____

Repairman contact info _____

Notes

Brand _____ Date _____

Purchased From _____ Price $ _____

Repairs _____

Repairs made by: _____

Repairman contact info _____

Notes

Cooktop

Brand _____ Date _____ ☐ Electric ☐ Gas ☐ LP ☐ Natural

Purchased From _____ Price $ _____

Installed by _____

Repairs _____

Repairs made by: _____

Repairman contact info _____

Notes:

Brand _____ Date _____

Purchased From _____ Price $ _____

Repairs _____

_____

Repairs made by: _____

Repairman contact info _____

Notes:

Oven

Brand _____ Date _____

Purchased From _____ Price $ _____

Installed by _____

Repairs _____

Repairs made by: _____

Repairman contact info

Notes

Brand _____ Date _____

Purchased From _____ Price $ _____

Repairs _____

Repairs made by: _____

Repairman contact info

Notes

Oven

Brand _____ Date _____

Purchased From _____ Price $ _____

Installed by _____

Repairs _____

Repairs made by: _____

Repairman contact info _____

```
Notes



```

Brand _____ Date _____

Purchased From _____ Price $ _____

Repairs _____

_____

Repairs made by: _____

Repairman contact info _____

```
Notes



```

Oven

Brand _____ Date _____

Purchased From _____ Price $ _____

Installed by _____

Repairs _____

Repairs made by: _____

Repairman contact info _____

Notes
```
                                                              
                                                              
                                                              
                                                              
```

Brand _____ Date _____

Purchased From _____ Price $ _____

Repairs _____

_____

Repairs made by: _____

Repairman contact info _____

Notes
```
                                                              
                                                              
                                                              
                                                              
```

Microwave

Brand _____ Date _____

Purchased From _____ Price $ _____

Installed by _____

Repairs _____

Repairs made by: _____

Repairman contact info _____

Notes

Brand _____ Date _____

Purchased From _____ Price $ _____

Repairs _____

Repairs made by: _____

Repairman contact info _____

Notes

Microwave left with house? ☐ YES ☐ NO

Microwave

Brand _____ Date _____

Purchased From _____ Price $ _____

Installed by _____

Repairs _____

Repairs made by: _____

Repairman contact info _____

Notes

Brand _____ Date _____

Purchased From _____ Price $ _____

Repairs _____

_____

Repairs made by: _____

Repairman contact info _____

Notes

Microwave left with house? ☐ YES ☐ NO

Microwave

Brand _____ Date _____

Purchased From _____ Price $ _____

Installed by _____

Repairs _____

Repairs made by: _____

Repairman contact info _____

Notes

Brand _____ Date _____

Purchased From _____ Price $ _____

Repairs _____

_____

Repairs made by: _____

Repairman contact info _____

Notes

Microwave left with house? ☐ YES ☐ NO

Microwave

Brand _____ Date _____

Purchased From _____ Price $ _____

Installed by _____

Repairs _____

Repairs made by: _____

Repairman contact info _____

Notes
```



```

Brand _____ Date _____

Purchased From _____ Price $ _____

Repairs _____

_____

Repairs made by: _____

Repairman contact info _____

Notes
```



```

Microwave left with house?   ☐ YES   ☐ NO

Dishwasher

Brand _____ Date _____

Purchased From _____ Price $ _____

Installed by _____

Repairs _____

Repairs made by: _____

Repairman contact info _____

Notes

Brand _____ Date _____

Purchased From _____ Price $ _____

Repairs _____

_____

Repairs made by: _____

Repairman contact info _____

Notes

Dishwasher

Brand _____ Date _____

Purchased From _____ Price $ _____

Installed by _____

Repairs _____

Repairs made by: _____

Repairman contact info _____

Notes

Brand _____ Date _____

Purchased From _____ Price $ _____

Repairs _____

_____

Repairs made by: _____

Repairman contact info _____

Notes

Dishwasher

Brand _____ Date _____

Purchased From _____ Price $ _____

Installed by _____

Repairs _____

Repairs made by: _____

Repairman contact info _____

Notes

Brand _____ Date _____

Purchased From _____ Price $ _____

Repairs _____

_____

Repairs made by: _____

Repairman contact info _____

Notes

Ice Maker

Brand _____ Date _____

Purchased From _____ Price $ _____

Installed by _____

Repairs _____

Repairs made by: _____

Repairman contact info _____

Notes

Brand _____ Date _____

Purchased From _____ Price $ _____

Repairs _____

Repairs made by: _____

Repairman contact info _____

Notes

Ice Maker

Brand _____ Date _____

Purchased From _____ Price $ _____

Installed by _____

Repairs _____

Repairs made by: _____

Repairman contact info _____

Notes

Brand _____ Date _____

Purchased From _____ Price $ _____

Repairs _____

_____

Repairs made by: _____

Repairman contact info _____

Notes

Trash Compactor

Brand _____ Date _____

Purchased From _____ Price $ _____

Installed by _____

Repairs _____

Repairs made by: _____

Repairman contact info

```
Notes



```

Brand _____ Date _____

Purchased From _____ Price $ _____

Repairs _____

_____

Repairs made by: _____

Repairman contact info

```
Notes



```

Trash Compactor

Brand _____ Date _____

Purchased From _____ Price $ _____

Installed by _____

Repairs _____

Repairs made by: _____

Repairman contact info _____

Notes

Brand _____ Date _____

Purchased From _____ Price $ _____

Repairs _____

_____

Repairs made by: _____

Repairman contact info _____

Notes

Freezer

Brand _____ Date _____

Purchased From _____ Price $ _____

Installed by _____

Repairs _____

Repairs made by: _____

Repairman contact info

Notes

Brand _____ Date _____

Purchased From _____ Price $ _____

Repairs _____

Repairs made by: _____

Repairman contact info

Notes

Freezer left with house? ☐ YES ☐ NO

Freezer

Brand _____ Date _____

Purchased From _____ Price $ _____

Installed by _____

Repairs _____

Repairs made by: _____

Repairman contact info _____

Notes
```




```

Brand _____ Date _____

Purchased From _____ Price $ _____

Repairs _____

_____

Repairs made by: _____

Repairman contact info _____

Notes
```




```

Freezer left with house? ☐ YES ☐ NO

Vent Hood

Brand _____ Date _____

Purchased From _____ Price $ _____

Installed by _____

Repairs _____

Repairs made by: _____

Repairman contact info

Notes

Brand _____ Date _____

Purchased From _____ Price $ _____

Repairs _____

_____

Repairs made by: _____

Repairman contact info

Notes

Vent Hood

Brand _____ Date _____

Purchased From _____ Price $ _____

Installed by _____

Repairs _____

Repairs made by: _____

Repairman contact info _____

Notes

Brand _____ Date _____

Purchased From _____ Price $ _____

Repairs _____

Repairs made by: _____

Repairman contact info _____

Notes

Water Heater

Brand _____ Date _____

Purchased From _____ Price $ _____

Installed by _____

Repairs _____

Repairs made by: _____

Repairman contact info _____

Notes
```

```

Brand _____ Date _____

Purchased From _____ Price $ _____

Repairs _____

_____

Repairs made by: _____

Repairman contact info _____

Notes

Water Heater

Brand _____ Date _____

Purchased From _____ Price $ _____

Installed by _____

Repairs _____

Repairs made by: _____

Repairman contact info _____

Notes

Brand _____ Date _____

Purchased From _____ Price $ _____

Repairs _____

_____

Repairs made by: _____

Repairman contact info _____

Notes

Water Heater

Brand _____ Date _____

Purchased From _____ Price $ _____

Installed by _____

Repairs _____

Repairs made by: _____

Repairman contact info

Notes

Brand _____ Date _____

Purchased From _____ Price $ _____

Repairs _____

Repairs made by: _____

Repairman contact info

Notes

Washer

Brand _____ Date _____

Purchased From _____ Price $ _____

Installed by _____

Repairs _____

Repairs made by: _____

Repairman contact info _____

Notes
```



```

Brand _____ Date _____

Purchased From _____ Price $ _____

Repairs _____

_____

Repairs made by: _____

Repairman contact info _____

Notes
```



```

Washer left with house? ☐ YES ☐ NO

Washer

Brand _____ Date _____

Purchased From _____ Price $ _____

Installed by _____

Repairs _____

Repairs made by: _____

Repairman contact info _____

Notes
```




```

Brand _____ Date _____

Purchased From _____ Price $ _____

Repairs _____

_____

Repairs made by: _____

Repairman contact info _____

Notes
```




```

Washer left with house? ☐ YES ☐ NO

Washer

Brand _____ Date _____

Purchased From _____ Price $ _____

Installed by _____

Repairs _____

Repairs made by: _____

Repairman contact info _____

Notes
```
┌─────────────────────────────────────────────┐
│                                             │
│                                             │
│                                             │
│                                             │
└─────────────────────────────────────────────┘
```

Brand _____ Date _____

Purchased From _____ Price $ _____

Repairs _____

_____

Repairs made by: _____

Repairman contact info _____

Notes
```
┌─────────────────────────────────────────────┐
│                                             │
│                                             │
│                                             │
│                                             │
└─────────────────────────────────────────────┘
```

Washer left with house?   ☐ YES   ☐ NO

Dryer

Brand _____ Date _____ ☐ Electric ☐ Gas ☐ LP ☐ Natural

Purchased From _____ Price $ _____

Installed by _____

Repairs _____

Repairs made by: _____

Repairman contact info _____

Notes
```



```

Brand _____ Date _____

Purchased From _____ Price $ _____

Repairs _____

_____

Repairs made by: _____

Repairman contact info _____

Notes
```



```

Dryer left with house? ☐ YES ☐ NO

Dryer

Brand _____ Date _____ ☐ Electric ☐ Gas ☐ LP ☐ Natural

Purchased From _____ Price $ _____

Installed by _____

Repairs _____

Repairs made by: _____

Repairman contact info _____

Notes

Brand _____ Date _____

Purchased From _____ Price $ _____

Repairs _____
_____

Repairs made by: _____

Repairman contact info _____

Notes

Dryer left with house?   ☐ YES   ☐ NO

Dryer

Brand _____ Date _____ ☐ Electric ☐ Gas ☐ LP ☐ Natural

Purchased From _____ Price $ _____

Installed by _____

Repairs _____

Repairs made by: _____

Repairman contact info _____

Notes

Brand _____ Date _____

Purchased From _____ Price $ _____

Repairs _____

_____

Repairs made by: _____

Repairman contact info _____

Notes

Dryer left with house? ☐ YES ☐ NO

Miscellaneous

Brand _____ Date _____

Item Description _____

Purchased From _____ Price $ _____

Installed by _____

Repairs _____

Repairman contact info _____

Notes
```


```

Brand _____ Date _____

Item Description _____

Purchased From _____ Price $ _____

Installed by _____

Repairs _____

Repairman contact info _____

Notes
```


```

Miscellaneous

Brand _____ Date _____

Item Description _____

Purchased From _____ Price $ _____

Installed by _____

Repairs _____

Repairman contact info _____

Notes
```



```

Brand _____ Date _____

Item Description _____

Purchased From _____ Price $ _____

Installed by _____

Repairs _____

Repairman contact info _____

Notes
```



```

Miscellaneous

Brand _____ Date _____

Item Description _____

Purchased From _____ Price $ _____

Installed by _____

Repairs _____

Repairman contact info _____

Notes
```
```

Brand _____ Date _____

Item Description _____

Purchased From _____ Price $ _____

Installed by _____

Repairs _____

Repairman contact info _____

Notes

Miscellaneous

Brand _____ Date _____

Item Description _____

Purchased From _____ Price $ _____

Installed by _____

Repairs _____

Repairman contact info _____

Notes

Brand _____ Date _____

Item Description _____

Purchased From _____ Price $ _____

Installed by _____

Repairs _____

Repairman contact info _____

Notes

Miscellaneous

Brand _____ Date _____

Item Description _____

Purchased From _____ Price $ _____

Installed by _____

Repairs _____

Repairman contact info _____

Notes

Brand _____ Date _____

Item Description _____

Purchased From _____ Price $ _____

Installed by _____

Repairs _____

Repairman contact info _____

Notes

Painting

Fun Fact
Paints began to be used in pre-historic times. The first pre-prepared, in-the-can paint was introduced by Sherwin-Williams in 1866.

Helpful Hint
Paint should always be stored in a dry location where it will be protected from freezing.

Room Name

Date Painted | **Paint Brand**

Painted by

Painters Contact Info

Wall Color	☐ Flat ☐ Matte ☐ Eggshell	☐ Satin ☐ Semi gloss ☐ High gloss
Ceiling Color	☐ Flat ☐ Matte ☐ Eggshell	☐ Satin ☐ Semi gloss ☐ High gloss
Trim Color	☐ Flat ☐ Matte ☐ Eggshell	☐ Satin ☐ Semi gloss ☐ High gloss

Notes

Room Name

Date Painted | **Paint Brand**

Painted by

Painters Contact Info

Wall Color	☐ Flat ☐ Matte ☐ Eggshell	☐ Satin ☐ Semi gloss ☐ High gloss
Ceiling Color	☐ Flat ☐ Matte ☐ Eggshell	☐ Satin ☐ Semi gloss ☐ High gloss
Trim Color	☐ Flat ☐ Matte ☐ Eggshell	☐ Satin ☐ Semi gloss ☐ High gloss

Notes

Room Name

Date Painted _____ Paint Brand _____

Painted by _____

Painters Contact Info

Wall Color	☐ Flat ☐ Satin ☐ Matte ☐ Semi gloss ☐ Eggshell ☐ High gloss
Ceiling Color	☐ Flat ☐ Satin ☐ Matte ☐ Semi gloss ☐ Eggshell ☐ High gloss
Trim Color	☐ Flat ☐ Satin ☐ Matte ☐ Semi gloss ☐ Eggshell ☐ High gloss

Notes

Room Name

Date Painted _____ Paint Brand _____

Painted by _____

Painters Contact Info

Wall Color	☐ Flat ☐ Satin ☐ Matte ☐ Semi gloss ☐ Eggshell ☐ High gloss
Ceiling Color	☐ Flat ☐ Satin ☐ Matte ☐ Semi gloss ☐ Eggshell ☐ High gloss
Trim Color	☐ Flat ☐ Satin ☐ Matte ☐ Semi gloss ☐ Eggshell ☐ High gloss

Notes

Room Name

Date Painted   Paint Brand

Painted by

Painters Contact Info

Wall Color
- ☐ Flat   ☐ Satin
- ☐ Matte   ☐ Semi gloss
- ☐ Eggshell ☐ High gloss

Ceiling Color
- ☐ Flat   ☐ Satin
- ☐ Matte   ☐ Semi gloss
- ☐ Eggshell ☐ High gloss

Trim Color
- ☐ Flat   ☐ Satin
- ☐ Matte   ☐ Semi gloss
- ☐ Eggshell ☐ High gloss

Notes

Room Name

Date Painted   Paint Brand

Painted by

Painters Contact Info

Wall Color
- ☐ Flat   ☐ Satin
- ☐ Matte   ☐ Semi gloss
- ☐ Eggshell ☐ High gloss

Ceiling Color
- ☐ Flat   ☐ Satin
- ☐ Matte   ☐ Semi gloss
- ☐ Eggshell ☐ High gloss

Trim Color
- ☐ Flat   ☐ Satin
- ☐ Matte   ☐ Semi gloss
- ☐ Eggshell ☐ High gloss

Notes

Room Name

Date Painted | Paint Brand

Painted by

Painters Contact Info

Wall Color
- ☐ Flat ☐ Satin
- ☐ Matte ☐ Semi gloss
- ☐ Eggshell ☐ High gloss

Ceiling Color
- ☐ Flat ☐ Satin
- ☐ Matte ☐ Semi gloss
- ☐ Eggshell ☐ High gloss

Trim Color
- ☐ Flat ☐ Satin
- ☐ Matte ☐ Semi gloss
- ☐ Eggshell ☐ High gloss

Notes

Room Name

Date Painted | Paint Brand

Painted by

Painters Contact Info

Wall Color
- ☐ Flat ☐ Satin
- ☐ Matte ☐ Semi gloss
- ☐ Eggshell ☐ High gloss

Ceiling Color
- ☐ Flat ☐ Satin
- ☐ Matte ☐ Semi gloss
- ☐ Eggshell ☐ High gloss

Trim Color
- ☐ Flat ☐ Satin
- ☐ Matte ☐ Semi gloss
- ☐ Eggshell ☐ High gloss

Notes

Room Name

Date Painted   **Paint Brand**

Painted by

Painters Contact Info

Wall Color — ☐ Flat ☐ Satin ☐ Matte ☐ Semi gloss ☐ Eggshell ☐ High gloss

Ceiling Color — ☐ Flat ☐ Satin ☐ Matte ☐ Semi gloss ☐ Eggshell ☐ High gloss

Trim Color — ☐ Flat ☐ Satin ☐ Matte ☐ Semi gloss ☐ Eggshell ☐ High gloss

Notes

Room Name

Date Painted   **Paint Brand**

Painted by

Painters Contact Info

Wall Color — ☐ Flat ☐ Satin ☐ Matte ☐ Semi gloss ☐ Eggshell ☐ High gloss

Ceiling Color — ☐ Flat ☐ Satin ☐ Matte ☐ Semi gloss ☐ Eggshell ☐ High gloss

Trim Color — ☐ Flat ☐ Satin ☐ Matte ☐ Semi gloss ☐ Eggshell ☐ High gloss

Notes

Room Name

Date Painted | Paint Brand

Painted by

Painters Contact Info

Wall Color | ☐ Flat ☐ Satin
☐ Matte ☐ Semi gloss
☐ Eggshell ☐ High gloss

Ceiling Color | ☐ Flat ☐ Satin
☐ Matte ☐ Semi gloss
☐ Eggshell ☐ High gloss

Trim Color | ☐ Flat ☐ Satin
☐ Matte ☐ Semi gloss
☐ Eggshell ☐ High gloss

Notes

Room Name

Date Painted | Paint Brand

Painted by

Painters Contact Info

Wall Color | ☐ Flat ☐ Satin
☐ Matte ☐ Semi gloss
☐ Eggshell ☐ High gloss

Ceiling Color | ☐ Flat ☐ Satin
☐ Matte ☐ Semi gloss
☐ Eggshell ☐ High gloss

Trim Color | ☐ Flat ☐ Satin
☐ Matte ☐ Semi gloss
☐ Eggshell ☐ High gloss

Notes

Room Name

Date Painted _____ Paint Brand _____

Painted by _____

Painters Contact Info _____

Wall Color	☐ Flat ☐ Matte ☐ Eggshell	☐ Satin ☐ Semi gloss ☐ High gloss
Ceiling Color	☐ Flat ☐ Matte ☐ Eggshell	☐ Satin ☐ Semi gloss ☐ High gloss
Trim Color	☐ Flat ☐ Matte ☐ Eggshell	☐ Satin ☐ Semi gloss ☐ High gloss

Notes

Room Name

Date Painted _____ Paint Brand _____

Painted by _____

Painters Contact Info _____

Wall Color	☐ Flat ☐ Matte ☐ Eggshell	☐ Satin ☐ Semi gloss ☐ High gloss
Ceiling Color	☐ Flat ☐ Matte ☐ Eggshell	☐ Satin ☐ Semi gloss ☐ High gloss
Trim Color	☐ Flat ☐ Matte ☐ Eggshell	☐ Satin ☐ Semi gloss ☐ High gloss

Notes

Room Name

Date Painted	Paint Brand
Painted by	
Painters Contact Info	

Wall Color	☐ Flat ☐ Satin ☐ Matte ☐ Semi gloss ☐ Eggshell ☐ High gloss
Ceiling Color	☐ Flat ☐ Satin ☐ Matte ☐ Semi gloss ☐ Eggshell ☐ High gloss
Trim Color	☐ Flat ☐ Satin ☐ Matte ☐ Semi gloss ☐ Eggshell ☐ High gloss

Notes

Room Name

Date Painted	Paint Brand
Painted by	
Painters Contact Info	

Wall Color	☐ Flat ☐ Satin ☐ Matte ☐ Semi gloss ☐ Eggshell ☐ High gloss
Ceiling Color	☐ Flat ☐ Satin ☐ Matte ☐ Semi gloss ☐ Eggshell ☐ High gloss
Trim Color	☐ Flat ☐ Satin ☐ Matte ☐ Semi gloss ☐ Eggshell ☐ High gloss

Notes

Room Name

Date Painted | **Paint Brand**

Painted by

Painters Contact Info

Wall Color	☐ Flat ☐ Satin ☐ Matte ☐ Semi gloss ☐ Eggshell ☐ High gloss
Ceiling Color	☐ Flat ☐ Satin ☐ Matte ☐ Semi gloss ☐ Eggshell ☐ High gloss
Trim Color	☐ Flat ☐ Satin ☐ Matte ☐ Semi gloss ☐ Eggshell ☐ High gloss

Notes

Room Name

Date Painted | **Paint Brand**

Painted by

Painters Contact Info

Wall Color	☐ Flat ☐ Satin ☐ Matte ☐ Semi gloss ☐ Eggshell ☐ High gloss
Ceiling Color	☐ Flat ☐ Satin ☐ Matte ☐ Semi gloss ☐ Eggshell ☐ High gloss
Trim Color	☐ Flat ☐ Satin ☐ Matte ☐ Semi gloss ☐ Eggshell ☐ High gloss

Notes

Room Name

Date Painted _____ Paint Brand _____

Painted by _____

Painters Contact Info

Wall Color	☐ Flat ☐ Satin ☐ Matte ☐ Semi gloss ☐ Eggshell ☐ High gloss
Ceiling Color	☐ Flat ☐ Satin ☐ Matte ☐ Semi gloss ☐ Eggshell ☐ High gloss
Trim Color	☐ Flat ☐ Satin ☐ Matte ☐ Semi gloss ☐ Eggshell ☐ High gloss

Notes

Room Name

Date Painted _____ Paint Brand _____

Painted by _____

Painters Contact Info

Wall Color	☐ Flat ☐ Satin ☐ Matte ☐ Semi gloss ☐ Eggshell ☐ High gloss
Ceiling Color	☐ Flat ☐ Satin ☐ Matte ☐ Semi gloss ☐ Eggshell ☐ High gloss
Trim Color	☐ Flat ☐ Satin ☐ Matte ☐ Semi gloss ☐ Eggshell ☐ High gloss

Notes

Room Name

Date Painted | **Paint Brand**

Painted by

Painters Contact Info

Wall Color
- ☐ Flat ☐ Satin
- ☐ Matte ☐ Semi gloss
- ☐ Eggshell ☐ High gloss

Ceiling Color
- ☐ Flat ☐ Satin
- ☐ Matte ☐ Semi gloss
- ☐ Eggshell ☐ High gloss

Trim Color
- ☐ Flat ☐ Satin
- ☐ Matte ☐ Semi gloss
- ☐ Eggshell ☐ High gloss

Notes

Room Name

Date Painted | **Paint Brand**

Painted by

Painters Contact Info

Wall Color
- ☐ Flat ☐ Satin
- ☐ Matte ☐ Semi gloss
- ☐ Eggshell ☐ High gloss

Ceiling Color
- ☐ Flat ☐ Satin
- ☐ Matte ☐ Semi gloss
- ☐ Eggshell ☐ High gloss

Trim Color
- ☐ Flat ☐ Satin
- ☐ Matte ☐ Semi gloss
- ☐ Eggshell ☐ High gloss

Notes

Room Name

Date Painted | Paint Brand

Painted by

Painters Contact Info

Wall Color
- ☐ Flat ☐ Satin
- ☐ Matte ☐ Semi gloss
- ☐ Eggshell ☐ High gloss

Ceiling Color
- ☐ Flat ☐ Satin
- ☐ Matte ☐ Semi gloss
- ☐ Eggshell ☐ High gloss

Trim Color
- ☐ Flat ☐ Satin
- ☐ Matte ☐ Semi gloss
- ☐ Eggshell ☐ High gloss

Notes

Room Name

Date Painted | Paint Brand

Painted by

Painters Contact Info

Wall Color
- ☐ Flat ☐ Satin
- ☐ Matte ☐ Semi gloss
- ☐ Eggshell ☐ High gloss

Ceiling Color
- ☐ Flat ☐ Satin
- ☐ Matte ☐ Semi gloss
- ☐ Eggshell ☐ High gloss

Trim Color
- ☐ Flat ☐ Satin
- ☐ Matte ☐ Semi gloss
- ☐ Eggshell ☐ High gloss

Notes

Room Name

Date Painted _____ Paint Brand _____

Painted by _____

Painters Contact Info _____

Wall Color	☐ Flat ☐ Satin ☐ Matte ☐ Semi gloss ☐ Eggshell ☐ High gloss
Ceiling Color	☐ Flat ☐ Satin ☐ Matte ☐ Semi gloss ☐ Eggshell ☐ High gloss
Trim Color	☐ Flat ☐ Satin ☐ Matte ☐ Semi gloss ☐ Eggshell ☐ High gloss

Notes

Room Name

Date Painted _____ Paint Brand _____

Painted by _____

Painters Contact Info _____

Wall Color	☐ Flat ☐ Satin ☐ Matte ☐ Semi gloss ☐ Eggshell ☐ High gloss
Ceiling Color	☐ Flat ☐ Satin ☐ Matte ☐ Semi gloss ☐ Eggshell ☐ High gloss
Trim Color	☐ Flat ☐ Satin ☐ Matte ☐ Semi gloss ☐ Eggshell ☐ High gloss

Notes

Room Name

Date Painted Paint Brand

Painted by

Painters Contact Info

Wall Color ☐ Flat ☐ Satin
 ☐ Matte ☐ Semi gloss
 ☐ Eggshell ☐ High gloss

Ceiling Color ☐ Flat ☐ Satin
 ☐ Matte ☐ Semi gloss
 ☐ Eggshell ☐ High gloss

Trim Color ☐ Flat ☐ Satin
 ☐ Matte ☐ Semi gloss
 ☐ Eggshell ☐ High gloss

Notes

Room Name

Date Painted Paint Brand

Painted by

Painters Contact Info

Wall Color ☐ Flat ☐ Satin
 ☐ Matte ☐ Semi gloss
 ☐ Eggshell ☐ High gloss

Ceiling Color ☐ Flat ☐ Satin
 ☐ Matte ☐ Semi gloss
 ☐ Eggshell ☐ High gloss

Trim Color ☐ Flat ☐ Satin
 ☐ Matte ☐ Semi gloss
 ☐ Eggshell ☐ High gloss

Notes

Room Name

Date Painted   Paint Brand

Painted by

Painters Contact Info

Wall Color — ☐ Flat ☐ Matte ☐ Eggshell ☐ Satin ☐ Semi gloss ☐ High gloss

Ceiling Color — ☐ Flat ☐ Matte ☐ Eggshell ☐ Satin ☐ Semi gloss ☐ High gloss

Trim Color — ☐ Flat ☐ Matte ☐ Eggshell ☐ Satin ☐ Semi gloss ☐ High gloss

Notes

Room Name

Date Painted   Paint Brand

Painted by

Painters Contact Info

Wall Color — ☐ Flat ☐ Matte ☐ Eggshell ☐ Satin ☐ Semi gloss ☐ High gloss

Ceiling Color — ☐ Flat ☐ Matte ☐ Eggshell ☐ Satin ☐ Semi gloss ☐ High gloss

Trim Color — ☐ Flat ☐ Matte ☐ Eggshell ☐ Satin ☐ Semi gloss ☐ High gloss

Notes

Room Name

Date Painted   Paint Brand

Painted by

Painters Contact Info

Wall Color
- ☐ Flat   ☐ Satin
- ☐ Matte   ☐ Semi gloss
- ☐ Eggshell ☐ High gloss

Ceiling Color
- ☐ Flat   ☐ Satin
- ☐ Matte   ☐ Semi gloss
- ☐ Eggshell ☐ High gloss

Trim Color
- ☐ Flat   ☐ Satin
- ☐ Matte   ☐ Semi gloss
- ☐ Eggshell ☐ High gloss

Notes

Room Name

Date Painted   Paint Brand

Painted by

Painters Contact Info

Wall Color
- ☐ Flat   ☐ Satin
- ☐ Matte   ☐ Semi gloss
- ☐ Eggshell ☐ High gloss

Ceiling Color
- ☐ Flat   ☐ Satin
- ☐ Matte   ☐ Semi gloss
- ☐ Eggshell ☐ High gloss

Trim Color
- ☐ Flat   ☐ Satin
- ☐ Matte   ☐ Semi gloss
- ☐ Eggshell ☐ High gloss

Notes

Room Name

Date Painted   Paint Brand

Painted by

Painters Contact Info

Wall Color
- ☐ Flat   ☐ Satin
- ☐ Matte   ☐ Semi gloss
- ☐ Eggshell ☐ High gloss

Ceiling Color
- ☐ Flat   ☐ Satin
- ☐ Matte   ☐ Semi gloss
- ☐ Eggshell ☐ High gloss

Trim Color
- ☐ Flat   ☐ Satin
- ☐ Matte   ☐ Semi gloss
- ☐ Eggshell ☐ High gloss

Notes

Room Name

Date Painted   Paint Brand

Painted by

Painters Contact Info

Wall Color
- ☐ Flat   ☐ Satin
- ☐ Matte   ☐ Semi gloss
- ☐ Eggshell ☐ High gloss

Ceiling Color
- ☐ Flat   ☐ Satin
- ☐ Matte   ☐ Semi gloss
- ☐ Eggshell ☐ High gloss

Trim Color
- ☐ Flat   ☐ Satin
- ☐ Matte   ☐ Semi gloss
- ☐ Eggshell ☐ High gloss

Notes

Room Name

Date Painted   Paint Brand

Painted by

Painters Contact Info

Wall Color — ☐ Flat ☐ Satin ☐ Matte ☐ Semi gloss ☐ Eggshell ☐ High gloss

Ceiling Color — ☐ Flat ☐ Satin ☐ Matte ☐ Semi gloss ☐ Eggshell ☐ High gloss

Trim Color — ☐ Flat ☐ Satin ☐ Matte ☐ Semi gloss ☐ Eggshell ☐ High gloss

Notes

Room Name

Date Painted   Paint Brand

Painted by

Painters Contact Info

Wall Color — ☐ Flat ☐ Satin ☐ Matte ☐ Semi gloss ☐ Eggshell ☐ High gloss

Ceiling Color — ☐ Flat ☐ Satin ☐ Matte ☐ Semi gloss ☐ Eggshell ☐ High gloss

Trim Color — ☐ Flat ☐ Satin ☐ Matte ☐ Semi gloss ☐ Eggshell ☐ High gloss

Notes

Room Name

Date Painted | Paint Brand

Painted by

Painters Contact Info

Wall Color
- ☐ Flat ☐ Satin
- ☐ Matte ☐ Semi gloss
- ☐ Eggshell ☐ High gloss

Ceiling Color
- ☐ Flat ☐ Satin
- ☐ Matte ☐ Semi gloss
- ☐ Eggshell ☐ High gloss

Trim Color
- ☐ Flat ☐ Satin
- ☐ Matte ☐ Semi gloss
- ☐ Eggshell ☐ High gloss

Notes

Room Name

Date Painted | Paint Brand

Painted by

Painters Contact Info

Wall Color
- ☐ Flat ☐ Satin
- ☐ Matte ☐ Semi gloss
- ☐ Eggshell ☐ High gloss

Ceiling Color
- ☐ Flat ☐ Satin
- ☐ Matte ☐ Semi gloss
- ☐ Eggshell ☐ High gloss

Trim Color
- ☐ Flat ☐ Satin
- ☐ Matte ☐ Semi gloss
- ☐ Eggshell ☐ High gloss

Notes

Room Name

Date Painted   Paint Brand

Painted by

Painters Contact Info

Wall Color	☐ Flat ☐ Matte ☐ Eggshell	☐ Satin ☐ Semi gloss ☐ High gloss
Ceiling Color	☐ Flat ☐ Matte ☐ Eggshell	☐ Satin ☐ Semi gloss ☐ High gloss
Trim Color	☐ Flat ☐ Matte ☐ Eggshell	☐ Satin ☐ Semi gloss ☐ High gloss

Notes

Room Name

Date Painted   Paint Brand

Painted by

Painters Contact Info

Wall Color	☐ Flat ☐ Matte ☐ Eggshell	☐ Satin ☐ Semi gloss ☐ High gloss
Ceiling Color	☐ Flat ☐ Matte ☐ Eggshell	☐ Satin ☐ Semi gloss ☐ High gloss
Trim Color	☐ Flat ☐ Matte ☐ Eggshell	☐ Satin ☐ Semi gloss ☐ High gloss

Notes

Room Name

Date Painted   Paint Brand

Painted by

Painters Contact Info

Wall Color — ☐ Flat ☐ Matte ☐ Eggshell ☐ Satin ☐ Semi gloss ☐ High gloss

Ceiling Color — ☐ Flat ☐ Matte ☐ Eggshell ☐ Satin ☐ Semi gloss ☐ High gloss

Trim Color — ☐ Flat ☐ Matte ☐ Eggshell ☐ Satin ☐ Semi gloss ☐ High gloss

Notes

Room Name

Date Painted   Paint Brand

Painted by

Painters Contact Info

Wall Color — ☐ Flat ☐ Matte ☐ Eggshell ☐ Satin ☐ Semi gloss ☐ High gloss

Ceiling Color — ☐ Flat ☐ Matte ☐ Eggshell ☐ Satin ☐ Semi gloss ☐ High gloss

Trim Color — ☐ Flat ☐ Matte ☐ Eggshell ☐ Satin ☐ Semi gloss ☐ High gloss

Notes

Room Name

Date Painted   Paint Brand

Painted by

Painters Contact Info

Wall Color — ☐ Flat ☐ Satin ☐ Matte ☐ Semi gloss ☐ Eggshell ☐ High gloss

Ceiling Color — ☐ Flat ☐ Satin ☐ Matte ☐ Semi gloss ☐ Eggshell ☐ High gloss

Trim Color — ☐ Flat ☐ Satin ☐ Matte ☐ Semi gloss ☐ Eggshell ☐ High gloss

Notes

Room Name

Date Painted   Paint Brand

Painted by

Painters Contact Info

Wall Color — ☐ Flat ☐ Satin ☐ Matte ☐ Semi gloss ☐ Eggshell ☐ High gloss

Ceiling Color — ☐ Flat ☐ Satin ☐ Matte ☐ Semi gloss ☐ Eggshell ☐ High gloss

Trim Color — ☐ Flat ☐ Satin ☐ Matte ☐ Semi gloss ☐ Eggshell ☐ High gloss

Notes

Room Name

Date Painted _____ Paint Brand _____

Painted by _____

Painters Contact Info _____

Wall Color _____
- ☐ Flat   ☐ Satin
- ☐ Matte ☐ Semi gloss
- ☐ Eggshell ☐ High gloss

Ceiling Color _____
- ☐ Flat   ☐ Satin
- ☐ Matte ☐ Semi gloss
- ☐ Eggshell ☐ High gloss

Trim Color _____
- ☐ Flat   ☐ Satin
- ☐ Matte ☐ Semi gloss
- ☐ Eggshell ☐ High gloss

Notes

Room Name

Date Painted _____ Paint Brand _____

Painted by _____

Painters Contact Info _____

Wall Color _____
- ☐ Flat   ☐ Satin
- ☐ Matte ☐ Semi gloss
- ☐ Eggshell ☐ High gloss

Ceiling Color _____
- ☐ Flat   ☐ Satin
- ☐ Matte ☐ Semi gloss
- ☐ Eggshell ☐ High gloss

Trim Color _____
- ☐ Flat   ☐ Satin
- ☐ Matte ☐ Semi gloss
- ☐ Eggshell ☐ High gloss

Notes

Room Name

Date Painted _____ Paint Brand _____

Painted by _____

Painters Contact Info _____

Wall Color _____
- ☐ Flat
- ☐ Matte
- ☐ Eggshell
- ☐ Satin
- ☐ Semi gloss
- ☐ High gloss

Ceiling Color _____
- ☐ Flat
- ☐ Matte
- ☐ Eggshell
- ☐ Satin
- ☐ Semi gloss
- ☐ High gloss

Trim Color _____
- ☐ Flat
- ☐ Matte
- ☐ Eggshell
- ☐ Satin
- ☐ Semi gloss
- ☐ High gloss

Notes

Room Name

Date Painted _____ Paint Brand _____

Painted by _____

Painters Contact Info _____

Wall Color _____
- ☐ Flat
- ☐ Matte
- ☐ Eggshell
- ☐ Satin
- ☐ Semi gloss
- ☐ High gloss

Ceiling Color _____
- ☐ Flat
- ☐ Matte
- ☐ Eggshell
- ☐ Satin
- ☐ Semi gloss
- ☐ High gloss

Trim Color _____
- ☐ Flat
- ☐ Matte
- ☐ Eggshell
- ☐ Satin
- ☐ Semi gloss
- ☐ High gloss

Notes

Room Name

Date Painted | Paint Brand

Painted by

Painters Contact Info

Wall Color
- ☐ Flat ☐ Satin
- ☐ Matte ☐ Semi gloss
- ☐ Eggshell ☐ High gloss

Ceiling Color
- ☐ Flat ☐ Satin
- ☐ Matte ☐ Semi gloss
- ☐ Eggshell ☐ High gloss

Trim Color
- ☐ Flat ☐ Satin
- ☐ Matte ☐ Semi gloss
- ☐ Eggshell ☐ High gloss

Notes

Room Name

Date Painted | Paint Brand

Painted by

Painters Contact Info

Wall Color
- ☐ Flat ☐ Satin
- ☐ Matte ☐ Semi gloss
- ☐ Eggshell ☐ High gloss

Ceiling Color
- ☐ Flat ☐ Satin
- ☐ Matte ☐ Semi gloss
- ☐ Eggshell ☐ High gloss

Trim Color
- ☐ Flat ☐ Satin
- ☐ Matte ☐ Semi gloss
- ☐ Eggshell ☐ High gloss

Notes

Room Name

Date Painted   Paint Brand

Painted by

Painters Contact Info

Wall Color
- ☐ Flat   ☐ Satin
- ☐ Matte   ☐ Semi gloss
- ☐ Eggshell   ☐ High gloss

Ceiling Color
- ☐ Flat   ☐ Satin
- ☐ Matte   ☐ Semi gloss
- ☐ Eggshell   ☐ High gloss

Trim Color
- ☐ Flat   ☐ Satin
- ☐ Matte   ☐ Semi gloss
- ☐ Eggshell   ☐ High gloss

Notes

Room Name

Date Painted   Paint Brand

Painted by

Painters Contact Info

Wall Color
- ☐ Flat   ☐ Satin
- ☐ Matte   ☐ Semi gloss
- ☐ Eggshell   ☐ High gloss

Ceiling Color
- ☐ Flat   ☐ Satin
- ☐ Matte   ☐ Semi gloss
- ☐ Eggshell   ☐ High gloss

Trim Color
- ☐ Flat   ☐ Satin
- ☐ Matte   ☐ Semi gloss
- ☐ Eggshell   ☐ High gloss

Notes

Room Name

Date Painted | **Paint Brand**

Painted by

Painters Contact Info

Wall Color	☐ Flat ☐ Matte ☐ Eggshell	☐ Satin ☐ Semi gloss ☐ High gloss
Ceiling Color	☐ Flat ☐ Matte ☐ Eggshell	☐ Satin ☐ Semi gloss ☐ High gloss
Trim Color	☐ Flat ☐ Matte ☐ Eggshell	☐ Satin ☐ Semi gloss ☐ High gloss

Notes

Room Name

Date Painted | **Paint Brand**

Painted by

Painters Contact Info

Wall Color	☐ Flat ☐ Matte ☐ Eggshell	☐ Satin ☐ Semi gloss ☐ High gloss
Ceiling Color	☐ Flat ☐ Matte ☐ Eggshell	☐ Satin ☐ Semi gloss ☐ High gloss
Trim Color	☐ Flat ☐ Matte ☐ Eggshell	☐ Satin ☐ Semi gloss ☐ High gloss

Notes

Room Name

Date Painted   Paint Brand

Painted by

Painters Contact Info

Wall Color	☐ Flat ☐ Matte ☐ Eggshell	☐ Satin ☐ Semi gloss ☐ High gloss
Ceiling Color	☐ Flat ☐ Matte ☐ Eggshell	☐ Satin ☐ Semi gloss ☐ High gloss
Trim Color	☐ Flat ☐ Matte ☐ Eggshell	☐ Satin ☐ Semi gloss ☐ High gloss

Notes

Room Name

Date Painted   Paint Brand

Painted by

Painters Contact Info

Wall Color	☐ Flat ☐ Matte ☐ Eggshell	☐ Satin ☐ Semi gloss ☐ High gloss
Ceiling Color	☐ Flat ☐ Matte ☐ Eggshell	☐ Satin ☐ Semi gloss ☐ High gloss
Trim Color	☐ Flat ☐ Matte ☐ Eggshell	☐ Satin ☐ Semi gloss ☐ High gloss

Notes

Room Name

Date Painted | Paint Brand

Painted by

Painters Contact Info

Wall Color	☐ Flat ☐ Satin ☐ Matte ☐ Semi gloss ☐ Eggshell ☐ High gloss
Ceiling Color	☐ Flat ☐ Satin ☐ Matte ☐ Semi gloss ☐ Eggshell ☐ High gloss
Trim Color	☐ Flat ☐ Satin ☐ Matte ☐ Semi gloss ☐ Eggshell ☐ High gloss

Notes

Room Name

Date Painted | Paint Brand

Painted by

Painters Contact Info

Wall Color	☐ Flat ☐ Satin ☐ Matte ☐ Semi gloss ☐ Eggshell ☐ High gloss
Ceiling Color	☐ Flat ☐ Satin ☐ Matte ☐ Semi gloss ☐ Eggshell ☐ High gloss
Trim Color	☐ Flat ☐ Satin ☐ Matte ☐ Semi gloss ☐ Eggshell ☐ High gloss

Notes

Room Name

Date Painted   Paint Brand

Painted by

Painters Contact Info

Wall Color	☐ Flat ☐ Matte ☐ Eggshell	☐ Satin ☐ Semi gloss ☐ High gloss
Ceiling Color	☐ Flat ☐ Matte ☐ Eggshell	☐ Satin ☐ Semi gloss ☐ High gloss
Trim Color	☐ Flat ☐ Matte ☐ Eggshell	☐ Satin ☐ Semi gloss ☐ High gloss

Notes

Room Name

Date Painted   Paint Brand

Painted by

Painters Contact Info

Wall Color	☐ Flat ☐ Matte ☐ Eggshell	☐ Satin ☐ Semi gloss ☐ High gloss
Ceiling Color	☐ Flat ☐ Matte ☐ Eggshell	☐ Satin ☐ Semi gloss ☐ High gloss
Trim Color	☐ Flat ☐ Matte ☐ Eggshell	☐ Satin ☐ Semi gloss ☐ High gloss

Notes

Room Name

Date Painted   Paint Brand

Painted by

Painters Contact Info

Wall Color	☐ Flat ☐ Satin ☐ Matte ☐ Semi gloss ☐ Eggshell ☐ High gloss
Ceiling Color	☐ Flat ☐ Satin ☐ Matte ☐ Semi gloss ☐ Eggshell ☐ High gloss
Trim Color	☐ Flat ☐ Satin ☐ Matte ☐ Semi gloss ☐ Eggshell ☐ High gloss

Notes

Room Name

Date Painted   Paint Brand

Painted by

Painters Contact Info

Wall Color	☐ Flat ☐ Satin ☐ Matte ☐ Semi gloss ☐ Eggshell ☐ High gloss
Ceiling Color	☐ Flat ☐ Satin ☐ Matte ☐ Semi gloss ☐ Eggshell ☐ High gloss
Trim Color	☐ Flat ☐ Satin ☐ Matte ☐ Semi gloss ☐ Eggshell ☐ High gloss

Notes

Room Name

Date Painted _____ Paint Brand _____

Painted by _____

Painters Contact Info _____

Wall Color _____
- ☐ Flat   ☐ Satin
- ☐ Matte   ☐ Semi gloss
- ☐ Eggshell   ☐ High gloss

Ceiling Color _____
- ☐ Flat   ☐ Satin
- ☐ Matte   ☐ Semi gloss
- ☐ Eggshell   ☐ High gloss

Trim Color _____
- ☐ Flat   ☐ Satin
- ☐ Matte   ☐ Semi gloss
- ☐ Eggshell   ☐ High gloss

Notes

Room Name

Date Painted _____ Paint Brand _____

Painted by _____

Painters Contact Info _____

Wall Color _____
- ☐ Flat   ☐ Satin
- ☐ Matte   ☐ Semi gloss
- ☐ Eggshell   ☐ High gloss

Ceiling Color _____
- ☐ Flat   ☐ Satin
- ☐ Matte   ☐ Semi gloss
- ☐ Eggshell   ☐ High gloss

Trim Color _____
- ☐ Flat   ☐ Satin
- ☐ Matte   ☐ Semi gloss
- ☐ Eggshell   ☐ High gloss

Notes

Room Name

Date Painted _____ Paint Brand _____

Painted by _____

Painters Contact Info _____

Wall Color _____
- [ ] Flat
- [ ] Matte
- [ ] Eggshell
- [ ] Satin
- [ ] Semi gloss
- [ ] High gloss

Ceiling Color _____
- [ ] Flat
- [ ] Matte
- [ ] Eggshell
- [ ] Satin
- [ ] Semi gloss
- [ ] High gloss

Trim Color _____
- [ ] Flat
- [ ] Matte
- [ ] Eggshell
- [ ] Satin
- [ ] Semi gloss
- [ ] High gloss

Notes

Room Name

Date Painted _____ Paint Brand _____

Painted by _____

Painters Contact Info _____

Wall Color _____
- [ ] Flat
- [ ] Matte
- [ ] Eggshell
- [ ] Satin
- [ ] Semi gloss
- [ ] High gloss

Ceiling Color _____
- [ ] Flat
- [ ] Matte
- [ ] Eggshell
- [ ] Satin
- [ ] Semi gloss
- [ ] High gloss

Trim Color _____
- [ ] Flat
- [ ] Matte
- [ ] Eggshell
- [ ] Satin
- [ ] Semi gloss
- [ ] High gloss

Notes

Room Name

Date Painted   Paint Brand

Painted by

Painters Contact Info

Wall Color | ☐ Flat   ☐ Satin
           | ☐ Matte ☐ Semi gloss
           | ☐ Eggshell ☐ High gloss

Ceiling Color | ☐ Flat   ☐ Satin
              | ☐ Matte ☐ Semi gloss
              | ☐ Eggshell ☐ High gloss

Trim Color | ☐ Flat   ☐ Satin
           | ☐ Matte ☐ Semi gloss
           | ☐ Eggshell ☐ High gloss

Notes

Room Name

Date Painted   Paint Brand

Painted by

Painters Contact Info

Wall Color | ☐ Flat   ☐ Satin
           | ☐ Matte ☐ Semi gloss
           | ☐ Eggshell ☐ High gloss

Ceiling Color | ☐ Flat   ☐ Satin
              | ☐ Matte ☐ Semi gloss
              | ☐ Eggshell ☐ High gloss

Trim Color | ☐ Flat   ☐ Satin
           | ☐ Matte ☐ Semi gloss
           | ☐ Eggshell ☐ High gloss

Notes

Room Name

Date Painted _____ Paint Brand _____

Painted by _____

Painters Contact Info _____

Wall Color	☐ Flat ☐ Matte ☐ Eggshell	☐ Satin ☐ Semi gloss ☐ High gloss
Ceiling Color	☐ Flat ☐ Matte ☐ Eggshell	☐ Satin ☐ Semi gloss ☐ High gloss
Trim Color	☐ Flat ☐ Matte ☐ Eggshell	☐ Satin ☐ Semi gloss ☐ High gloss

Notes

Room Name

Date Painted _____ Paint Brand _____

Painted by _____

Painters Contact Info _____

Wall Color	☐ Flat ☐ Matte ☐ Eggshell	☐ Satin ☐ Semi gloss ☐ High gloss
Ceiling Color	☐ Flat ☐ Matte ☐ Eggshell	☐ Satin ☐ Semi gloss ☐ High gloss
Trim Color	☐ Flat ☐ Matte ☐ Eggshell	☐ Satin ☐ Semi gloss ☐ High gloss

Notes

Room Name

Date Painted | Paint Brand

Painted by

Painters Contact Info

Wall Color
- ☐ Flat   ☐ Satin
- ☐ Matte   ☐ Semi gloss
- ☐ Eggshell ☐ High gloss

Ceiling Color
- ☐ Flat   ☐ Satin
- ☐ Matte   ☐ Semi gloss
- ☐ Eggshell ☐ High gloss

Trim Color
- ☐ Flat   ☐ Satin
- ☐ Matte   ☐ Semi gloss
- ☐ Eggshell ☐ High gloss

Notes

Room Name

Date Painted | Paint Brand

Painted by

Painters Contact Info

Wall Color
- ☐ Flat   ☐ Satin
- ☐ Matte   ☐ Semi gloss
- ☐ Eggshell ☐ High gloss

Ceiling Color
- ☐ Flat   ☐ Satin
- ☐ Matte   ☐ Semi gloss
- ☐ Eggshell ☐ High gloss

Trim Color
- ☐ Flat   ☐ Satin
- ☐ Matte   ☐ Semi gloss
- ☐ Eggshell ☐ High gloss

Notes

Room Name

Date Painted _____ Paint Brand _____

Painted by _____

Painters Contact Info _____

Wall Color	☐ Flat ☐ Satin ☐ Matte ☐ Semi gloss ☐ Eggshell ☐ High gloss
Ceiling Color	☐ Flat ☐ Satin ☐ Matte ☐ Semi gloss ☐ Eggshell ☐ High gloss
Trim Color	☐ Flat ☐ Satin ☐ Matte ☐ Semi gloss ☐ Eggshell ☐ High gloss

Notes

Room Name

Date Painted _____ Paint Brand _____

Painted by _____

Painters Contact Info _____

Wall Color	☐ Flat ☐ Satin ☐ Matte ☐ Semi gloss ☐ Eggshell ☐ High gloss
Ceiling Color	☐ Flat ☐ Satin ☐ Matte ☐ Semi gloss ☐ Eggshell ☐ High gloss
Trim Color	☐ Flat ☐ Satin ☐ Matte ☐ Semi gloss ☐ Eggshell ☐ High gloss

Notes

Room Name

Date Painted _____ Paint Brand _____

Painted by _____

Painters Contact Info

Wall Color	☐ Flat ☐ Satin ☐ Matte ☐ Semi gloss ☐ Eggshell ☐ High gloss
Ceiling Color	☐ Flat ☐ Satin ☐ Matte ☐ Semi gloss ☐ Eggshell ☐ High gloss
Trim Color	☐ Flat ☐ Satin ☐ Matte ☐ Semi gloss ☐ Eggshell ☐ High gloss

Notes

Room Name

Date Painted _____ Paint Brand _____

Painted by _____

Painters Contact Info

Wall Color	☐ Flat ☐ Satin ☐ Matte ☐ Semi gloss ☐ Eggshell ☐ High gloss
Ceiling Color	☐ Flat ☐ Satin ☐ Matte ☐ Semi gloss ☐ Eggshell ☐ High gloss
Trim Color	☐ Flat ☐ Satin ☐ Matte ☐ Semi gloss ☐ Eggshell ☐ High gloss

Notes

Room Name

Date Painted | **Paint Brand**

Painted by

Painters Contact Info

Wall Color
- ☐ Flat   ☐ Satin
- ☐ Matte   ☐ Semi gloss
- ☐ Eggshell ☐ High gloss

Ceiling Color
- ☐ Flat   ☐ Satin
- ☐ Matte   ☐ Semi gloss
- ☐ Eggshell ☐ High gloss

Trim Color
- ☐ Flat   ☐ Satin
- ☐ Matte   ☐ Semi gloss
- ☐ Eggshell ☐ High gloss

Notes

Room Name

Date Painted | **Paint Brand**

Painted by

Painters Contact Info

Wall Color
- ☐ Flat   ☐ Satin
- ☐ Matte   ☐ Semi gloss
- ☐ Eggshell ☐ High gloss

Ceiling Color
- ☐ Flat   ☐ Satin
- ☐ Matte   ☐ Semi gloss
- ☐ Eggshell ☐ High gloss

Trim Color
- ☐ Flat   ☐ Satin
- ☐ Matte   ☐ Semi gloss
- ☐ Eggshell ☐ High gloss

Notes

Room Name

Date Painted _____ Paint Brand _____

Painted by _____

Painters Contact Info _____

Wall Color	☐ Flat ☐ Matte ☐ Eggshell	☐ Satin ☐ Semi gloss ☐ High gloss
Ceiling Color	☐ Flat ☐ Matte ☐ Eggshell	☐ Satin ☐ Semi gloss ☐ High gloss
Trim Color	☐ Flat ☐ Matte ☐ Eggshell	☐ Satin ☐ Semi gloss ☐ High gloss

Notes

Room Name

Date Painted _____ Paint Brand _____

Painted by _____

Painters Contact Info _____

Wall Color	☐ Flat ☐ Matte ☐ Eggshell	☐ Satin ☐ Semi gloss ☐ High gloss
Ceiling Color	☐ Flat ☐ Matte ☐ Eggshell	☐ Satin ☐ Semi gloss ☐ High gloss
Trim Color	☐ Flat ☐ Matte ☐ Eggshell	☐ Satin ☐ Semi gloss ☐ High gloss

Notes

Room Name

Date Painted _____ **Paint Brand** _____

Painted by _____

Painters Contact Info _____

Wall Color _____
- ☐ Flat   ☐ Satin
- ☐ Matte   ☐ Semi gloss
- ☐ Eggshell ☐ High gloss

Ceiling Color _____
- ☐ Flat   ☐ Satin
- ☐ Matte   ☐ Semi gloss
- ☐ Eggshell ☐ High gloss

Trim Color _____
- ☐ Flat   ☐ Satin
- ☐ Matte   ☐ Semi gloss
- ☐ Eggshell ☐ High gloss

Notes

Room Name

Date Painted _____ **Paint Brand** _____

Painted by _____

Painters Contact Info _____

Wall Color _____
- ☐ Flat   ☐ Satin
- ☐ Matte   ☐ Semi gloss
- ☐ Eggshell ☐ High gloss

Ceiling Color _____
- ☐ Flat   ☐ Satin
- ☐ Matte   ☐ Semi gloss
- ☐ Eggshell ☐ High gloss

Trim Color _____
- ☐ Flat   ☐ Satin
- ☐ Matte   ☐ Semi gloss
- ☐ Eggshell ☐ High gloss

Notes

Floor Covering

Fun Fact
The weaving of carpets and rugs originated in Persia and dates to the Bronze Age!

Helpful Hint
Always check your manufacturer's info before using any cleaning product on your flooring.
Not only can they be ineffective,
but may permanently damage your floor.

Floor Covering

Room Name   Date Installed

Flooring Type *i.e. carpet, wood*

Purchased from   Price $

Installed by

Installers Contact Info

Notes

Room Name   Date Installed

Flooring Type *i.e. carpet, wood*

Purchased from   Price $

Installed by

Installers Contact Info

Notes

Room Name   Date Installed

Flooring Type *i.e. carpet, wood*

Purchased from   Price $

Installed by

Installers Contact Info

Notes

Floor Covering

Room Name _____ Date Installed _____

Flooring Type *i.e. carpet, wood* _____

Purchased from _____ Price $ _____

Installed by _____

Installers Contact Info _____

Notes

Room Name _____ Date Installed _____

Flooring Type *i.e. carpet, wood* _____

Purchased from _____ Price $ _____

Installed by _____

Installers Contact Info _____

Notes

Room Name _____ Date Installed _____

Flooring Type *i.e. carpet, wood* _____

Purchased from _____ Price $ _____

Installed by _____

Installers Contact Info _____

Notes

Floor Covering

Room Name _____ Date Installed _____

Flooring Type *i.e. carpet, wood* _____

Purchased from _____ Price $ _____

Installed by _____

Installers Contact Info _____

Notes

Room Name _____ Date Installed _____

Flooring Type *i.e. carpet, wood* _____

Purchased from _____ Price $ _____

Installed by _____

Installers Contact Info _____

Notes

Room Name _____ Date Installed _____

Flooring Type *i.e. carpet, wood* _____

Purchased from _____ Price $ _____

Installed by _____

Installers Contact Info _____

Notes

Floor Covering

Room Name _____ Date Installed _____

Flooring Type *i.e. carpet, wood* _____

Purchased from _____ Price $ _____

Installed by _____

Installers Contact Info _____

Notes

Room Name _____ Date Installed _____

Flooring Type *i.e. carpet, wood* _____

Purchased from _____ Price $ _____

Installed by _____

Installers Contact Info _____

Notes

Room Name _____ Date Installed _____

Flooring Type *i.e. carpet, wood* _____

Purchased from _____ Price $ _____

Installed by _____

Installers Contact Info _____

Notes

Floor Covering

Room Name _____ Date Installed _____

Flooring Type *i.e. carpet, wood* _____

Purchased from _____ Price $ _____

Installed by _____

Installers Contact Info _____

Notes

Room Name _____ Date Installed _____

Flooring Type *i.e. carpet, wood* _____

Purchased from _____ Price $ _____

Installed by _____

Installers Contact Info _____

Notes

Room Name _____ Date Installed _____

Flooring Type *i.e. carpet, wood* _____

Purchased from _____ Price $ _____

Installed by _____

Installers Contact Info _____

Notes

Floor Covering

Room Name   Date Installed

Flooring Type *i.e. carpet, wood*

Purchased from   Price $

Installed by

Installers Contact Info

Notes

Room Name   Date Installed

Flooring Type *i.e. carpet, wood*

Purchased from   Price $

Installed by

Installers Contact Info

Notes

Room Name   Date Installed

Flooring Type *i.e. carpet, wood*

Purchased from   Price $

Installed by

Installers Contact Info

Notes

Floor Covering

Room Name   Date Installed

Flooring Type *i.e. carpet, wood*

Purchased from   Price $

Installed by

Installers Contact Info

Notes

Room Name   Date Installed

Flooring Type *i.e. carpet, wood*

Purchased from   Price $

Installed by

Installers Contact Info

Notes

Room Name   Date Installed

Flooring Type *i.e. carpet, wood*

Purchased from   Price $

Installed by

Installers Contact Info

Notes

Floor Covering

Room Name   Date Installed

Flooring Type *i.e. carpet, wood*

Purchased from   Price $

Installed by

Installers Contact Info

Notes

Room Name   Date Installed

Flooring Type *i.e. carpet, wood*

Purchased from   Price $

Installed by

Installers Contact Info

Notes

Room Name   Date Installed

Flooring Type *i.e. carpet, wood*

Purchased from   Price $

Installed by

Installers Contact Info

Notes

Floor Covering

Room Name _____ Date Installed _____

Flooring Type *i.e. carpet, wood* _____

Purchased from _____ Price $ _____

Installed by _____

Installers Contact Info _____

Notes

Room Name _____ Date Installed _____

Flooring Type *i.e. carpet, wood* _____

Purchased from _____ Price $ _____

Installed by _____

Installers Contact Info _____

Notes

Room Name _____ Date Installed _____

Flooring Type *i.e. carpet, wood* _____

Purchased from _____ Price $ _____

Installed by _____

Installers Contact Info _____

Notes

Floor Covering

Room Name   Date Installed

Flooring Type *i.e. carpet, wood*

Purchased from   Price $

Installed by

Installers Contact Info

Notes

Room Name   Date Installed

Flooring Type *i.e. carpet, wood*

Purchased from   Price $

Installed by

Installers Contact Info

Notes

Room Name   Date Installed

Flooring Type *i.e. carpet, wood*

Purchased from   Price $

Installed by

Installers Contact Info

Notes

Floor Covering

Room Name _____ Date Installed _____

Flooring Type *i.e. carpet, wood* _____

Purchased from _____ Price $ _____

Installed by _____

Installers Contact Info _____

Notes
_____

Room Name _____ Date Installed _____

Flooring Type *i.e. carpet, wood* _____

Purchased from _____ Price $ _____

Installed by _____

Installers Contact Info _____

Notes
_____

Room Name _____ Date Installed _____

Flooring Type *i.e. carpet, wood* _____

Purchased from _____ Price $ _____

Installed by _____

Installers Contact Info _____

Notes
_____

Floor Covering

Room Name _____ Date Installed _____

Flooring Type *i.e. carpet, wood* _____

Purchased from _____ Price $ _____

Installed by _____

Installers Contact Info _____

Notes

Room Name _____ Date Installed _____

Flooring Type *i.e. carpet, wood* _____

Purchased from _____ Price $ _____

Installed by _____

Installers Contact Info _____

Notes

Room Name _____ Date Installed _____

Flooring Type *i.e. carpet, wood* _____

Purchased from _____ Price $ _____

Installed by _____

Installers Contact Info _____

Notes

Floor Covering

Room Name Date Installed

Flooring Type *i.e. carpet, wood*

Purchased from Price $

Installed by

Installers Contact Info

Notes

Room Name Date Installed

Flooring Type *i.e. carpet, wood*

Purchased from Price $

Installed by

Installers Contact Info

Notes

Room Name Date Installed

Flooring Type *i.e. carpet, wood*

Purchased from Price $

Installed by

Installers Contact Info

Notes

Floor Covering

Room Name   Date Installed

Flooring Type *i.e. carpet, wood*

Purchased from   Price $

Installed by

Installers Contact Info

Notes

Room Name   Date Installed

Flooring Type *i.e. carpet, wood*

Purchased from   Price $

Installed by

Installers Contact Info

Notes

Room Name   Date Installed

Flooring Type *i.e. carpet, wood*

Purchased from   Price $

Installed by

Installers Contact Info

Notes

Floor Covering

Room Name   Date Installed

Flooring Type *i.e. carpet, wood*

Purchased from   Price $

Installed by

Installers Contact Info

Notes

Room Name   Date Installed

Flooring Type *i.e. carpet, wood*

Purchased from   Price $

Installed by

Installers Contact Info

Notes

Room Name   Date Installed

Flooring Type *i.e. carpet, wood*

Purchased from   Price $

Installed by

Installers Contact Info

Notes

Floor Covering

Room Name   Date Installed

Flooring Type *i.e. carpet, wood*

Purchased from   Price $

Installed by

Installers Contact Info

Notes

Room Name   Date Installed

Flooring Type *i.e. carpet, wood*

Purchased from   Price $

Installed by

Installers Contact Info

Notes

Room Name   Date Installed

Flooring Type *i.e. carpet, wood*

Purchased from   Price $

Installed by

Installers Contact Info

Notes

Floor Covering

Room Name Date Installed

Flooring Type *i.e. carpet, wood*

Purchased from   Price $

Installed by

Installers Contact Info

Notes

Room Name Date Installed

Flooring Type *i.e. carpet, wood*

Purchased from   Price $

Installed by

Installers Contact Info

Notes

Room Name Date Installed

Flooring Type *i.e. carpet, wood*

Purchased from   Price $

Installed by

Installers Contact Info

Notes

Floor Covering

Room Name _____ Date Installed _____

Flooring Type _i.e. carpet, wood_ _____

Purchased from _____ Price $ _____

Installed by _____

Installers Contact Info _____

Notes

Room Name _____ Date Installed _____

Flooring Type _i.e. carpet, wood_ _____

Purchased from _____ Price $ _____

Installed by _____

Installers Contact Info _____

Notes

Room Name _____ Date Installed _____

Flooring Type _i.e. carpet, wood_ _____

Purchased from _____ Price $ _____

Installed by _____

Installers Contact Info _____

Notes

Floor Covering

Room Name _____ Date Installed _____

Flooring Type *i.e. carpet, wood* _____

Purchased from _____ Price $ _____

Installed by _____

Installers Contact Info _____

Notes

Room Name _____ Date Installed _____

Flooring Type *i.e. carpet, wood* _____

Purchased from _____ Price $ _____

Installed by _____

Installers Contact Info _____

Notes

Room Name _____ Date Installed _____

Flooring Type *i.e. carpet, wood* _____

Purchased from _____ Price $ _____

Installed by _____

Installers Contact Info _____

Notes

EXTERIOR

Fun Fact
Ceramic, fired brick were in use in China as far back as the 4th millenia B.C.

Helpful Hint
Vinyl siding can be painted to give your house a fresh, new look. Appropriate cleaners for vinyl siding are available at your local paint and hardware stores.

Windows & Shutters

Windows

Brand _____ Color _____

Location of repaired window _____

Repairs _____ Date _____

Repairs made by: _____

Repairman contact info _____

Notes

Location of repaired window _____

Repairs _____ Date _____

Repairs made by: _____

Repairman contact info _____

Notes

Location of repaired window _____

Repairs _____ Date _____

Repairs made by: _____

Repairman contact info _____

Notes

Windows & Shutters

Windows

Brand _____ Color _____

Location of repaired window _____

Repairs _____ Date _____

Repairs made by: _____

Repairman contact info _____

Notes

Location of repaired window _____

Repairs _____ Date _____

Repairs made by: _____

Repairman contact info _____

Notes

Location of repaired window _____

Repairs _____ Date _____

Repairs made by: _____

Repairman contact info _____

Notes

Windows & Shutters

Shutters

☐ Louvre
☐ Raised Panel
☐ Other

Brand _____ Color _____

Location of repaired shutter _____

Repairs _____ Date _____

Repairs made by: _____

Repairman contact info _____

Notes

Location of repaired shutter _____

Repairs _____ Date _____

Repairs made by: _____

Repairman contact info _____

Notes

Location of repaired shutter _____

Repairs _____ Date _____

Repairs made by: _____

Repairman contact info _____

Notes

Windows & Shutters

☐ Louvre
☐ Raised Panel
☐ Other

Shutters

Brand _____ Color _____

Location of repaired shutter _____

Repairs _____ Date _____

Repairs made by: _____

Repairman contact info _____

Notes

Location of repaired shutter _____

Repairs _____ Date _____

Repairs made by: _____

Repairman contact info _____

Notes

Location of repaired shutter _____

Repairs _____ Date _____

Repairs made by: _____

Repairman contact info _____

Notes

DOORS

Brand _____ Color _____

Location of repaired door _____

Repairs _____ Date _____

Repairs made by: _____

Repairman contact info _____

```
Notes



```

Location of repaired door _____

Repairs _____ Date _____

Repairs made by: _____

Repairman contact info _____

```
Notes



```

Location of repaired door _____

Repairs _____ Date _____

Repairs made by: _____

Repairman contact info _____

```
Notes



```

DOORS

Brand _____ Color _____

Location of repaired door _____

Repairs _____ Date _____

Repairs made by: _____

Repairman contact info _____

Notes

Location of repaired door _____

Repairs _____ Date _____

Repairs made by: _____

Repairman contact info _____

Notes

Location of repaired door _____

Repairs _____ Date _____

Repairs made by: _____

Repairman contact info _____

Notes

Soffit & Gutters

Brand _____ Color _____

Original to the house ☐ Yes ☐ No

Changes made to style and color: _____

_____

_____

_____

_____

Changes made by: _____ Date _____

Location of repair _____

Repairs _____ Date _____

Repairs made by: _____

Repairman contact info _____

Notes

Location of repair _____

Repairs _____ Date _____

Repairs made by: _____

Repairman contact info _____

Notes

Brick & Rock

BRICK

Brand _____ Color _____

Original to the house ☐ Yes ☐ No

Changes made to style and color: _____

_____

_____

_____

_____

Changes made by: _____ Date _____

Location of repair _____

Repairs _____ Date _____

Repairs made by: _____

Repairman contact info _____

Notes

Location of repair _____

Repairs _____ Date _____

Repairs made by: _____

Repairman contact info _____

Notes

Brick & Rock

ROCK

Brand _____ Color _____

Original to the house   ☐ Yes   ☐ No

Changes made to style and color: _____

_____

_____

_____

Changes made by: _____ Date _____

Location of repair _____

Repairs _____ Date _____

Repairs made by: _____

Repairman contact info _____

Notes

Location of repair _____

Repairs _____ Date _____

Repairs made by: _____

Repairman contact info _____

Notes

Vinyl Siding

Brand _____ Color _____

Original to the house ☐ Yes ☐ No

Changes made to style and color:

_____

_____

_____

_____

Changes made by: _____ Date _____

Location of repair _____

Repairs _____ Date _____

Repairs made by: _____

Repairman contact info _____

Notes

Location of repair _____

Repairs _____ Date _____

Repairs made by: _____

Repairman contact info _____

Notes

Driveway & Sidewalks

Driveway

☐ Concrete ☐ Asphalt/Paved ☐ Brown Rock/Aggregate ☐ Gravel

Originally installed by: _____

Additional work: _____ Date _____

_____

_____

_____

Additional work done by: _____

Location of repair _____

Repairs _____ Date _____

Repairs made by: _____

Repairman contact info _____

Notes

Location of repair _____

Repairs _____ Date _____

Repairs made by: _____

Repairman contact info _____

Notes

Driveway & Sidewalks

Sidewalks

☐ Concrete   ☐ Stones   ☐ Brown Rock/Aggregate   ☐ Gravel

Originally installed by: _____

Additional work: _____ Date _____

_____

_____

Additional work done by: _____

Location of repair _____

Repairs _____ Date _____

Repairs made by: _____

Repairman contact info _____

Notes

Location of repair _____

Repairs _____ Date _____

Repairs made by: _____

Repairman contact info _____

Notes

Patios & Decks

Patios

☐ Concrete ☐ Brown Rock/Aggregate ☐ Stones

Originally installed by: _____

Additional work: _____ Date _____

_____

_____

_____

Additional work done by: _____

Location of repair _____

Repairs _____ Date _____

Repairs made by: _____

Repairman contact info _____

Notes

Location of repair _____

Repairs _____ Date _____

Repairs made by: _____

Repairman contact info _____

Notes

Patios & Decks

Decks

☐ Treated   ☐ Trex

Originally installed by: _____

Additional work: _____ Date _____

_____

_____

Additional work done by: _____

Location of repair _____

Repairs _____ Date _____

Repairs made by: _____

Repairman contact info _____

Notes

Location of repair _____

Repairs _____ Date _____

Repairs made by: _____

Repairman contact info _____

Notes

Roofing

Brand _____ Color _____

Style: (i.e. shingles, metal, architectural) _____

Original to the house _____ ☐ Yes ☐ No

Changes made to style and color: _____

_____

_____

Changes made by: _____ Date _____

Location of repair _____

Repairs _____ Date _____

Repairs made by: _____

Repairman contact info _____

Notes

Location of repair _____

Repairs _____ Date _____

Repairs made by: _____

Repairman contact info _____

Notes

Roof #2

Brand _____ Color _____

Style: (i.e. shingles, metal, architectural) _____

Original to the house ☐ Yes ☐ No

Changes made to style and color: _____
_____
_____

Changes made by: _____ Date _____

Location of repair _____

Repairs _____ Date _____

Repairs made by: _____

Repairman contact info _____

Notes

Location of repair _____

Repairs _____ Date _____

Repairs made by: _____

Repairman contact info _____

Notes

Roof #3

Brand _____ Color _____

Style: (i.e. shingles, metal, architectural) _____

Original to the house ☐ Yes ☐ No

Changes made to style and color: _____
_____
_____

Changes made by: _____ Date _____

Location of repair _____

Repairs _____ Date _____

Repairs made by: _____

Repairman contact info _____

Notes

Location of repair _____

Repairs _____ Date _____

Repairs made by: _____

Repairman contact info _____

Notes

Roof #4

Brand _____ Color _____

Style: (i.e. shingles, metal, architectural) _____

Original to the house ☐ Yes ☐ No

Changes made to style and color: _____

_____

_____

Changes made by: _____ Date _____

Location of repair _____

Repairs _____ Date _____

Repairs made by: _____

Repairman contact info _____

Notes

Location of repair _____

Repairs _____ Date _____

Repairs made by: _____

Repairman contact info _____

Notes

Landscaping

Original Landscaping by: _____ Date _____

Landscaping additions with dates: _____

_____

_____

_____

_____

_____

_____

_____

_____

_____

_____

_____

_____

_____

Landscaping

Original Landscaping by: _____ Date _____

Landscaping additions with dates: _____

_____

_____

_____

_____

_____

_____

_____

_____

_____

_____

_____

_____

_____

_____

_____

_____

Landscaping

Original Landscaping by: _____ Date _____

Landscaping additions with dates: _____

_____

_____

_____

_____

_____

_____

_____

_____

_____

_____

_____

_____

_____

_____

REMODELS

Remodel #1

Home Owner _____

Date remodel began _____ Date remodel finished _____

Contractor _____

If no contractor,
work performed by _____

_____

_____

_____

_____

Describe scope of work _____

_____

_____

_____

_____

_____

_____

Total Cost of Project _____

Notes

Remodel #2

Home Owner _____

Date remodel began _____ Date remodel finished _____

Contractor _____

If no contractor,
work performed by _____

_____

_____

_____

Describe scope of work _____

_____

_____

_____

_____

_____

_____

_____

Total Cost of Project _____

Notes

Remodel #3

Home Owner _____

Date remodel began _____ Date remodel finished _____

Contractor _____

If no contractor,
work performed by _____

_____

_____

_____

_____

Describe scope of work _____

_____

_____

_____

_____

_____

_____

_____

_____

Total Cost of Project _____

Notes

Remodel #4

Home Owner _____

Date remodel began _____ Date remodel finished _____

Contractor _____

If no contractor,
work performed by _____

_____

_____

_____

_____

Describe scope of work _____

_____

_____

_____

_____

_____

_____

_____

Total Cost of Project _____

Notes

Remodel #5

Home Owner

Date remodel began   Date remodel finished

Contractor

If no contractor,
work performed by

Describe scope of work

Total Cost of Project

Notes

Remodel #6

Home Owner

Date remodel began   Date remodel finished

Contractor

If no contractor,
work performed by

Describe scope of work

Total Cost of Project

Notes

Remodel #7

Home Owner

Date remodel began   Date remodel finished

Contractor

If no contractor,
work performed by

Describe scope of work

Total Cost of Project

Notes

www.ingramcontent.com/pod-product-compliance
Lightning Source LLC
Chambersburg PA
CBHW072007110526
44592CB00012B/1229